SINGER

SEWING REFERENCE LIBRARY™

Sewing for the Home

Cy DeCosse Incorporated
Minnetonka, Minnesota

SINGER

SEWING REFERENCE LIBRARY™

Sewing for the Home

Contents

Copyright © 1984, 1988
Cy DeCosse Incorporated
5900 Green Oak Drive
Minnetonka, Minnesota 55343
All rights reserved
Printed in U.S.A.

Also available from the publisher: *Sewing Essentials, Clothing Care & Repair, Sewing for Style, Sewing Specialty Fabrics, Sewing Activewear,* *The Perfect Fit, Timesaving Sewing, More Sewing for the Home, Sewing Update, Tailoring.*

Library of Congress Cataloging in Publication Data

Sewing for the Home

(Singer Sewing Reference Library)
Includes index.
1. Sewing 2. House Furnishings I. Series.
TT715.S48 1984 646.2'1 84-42638
ISBN 0-86573-203-5
ISBN 0-86573-204-3 (pbk.)

Distributed by: Contemporary Books, Inc., Chicago Illinois

CY DE COSSE INCORPORATED
Chairman: Cy DeCosse
President: James B. Maus
Executive Vice President: William B. Jones

SEWING FOR THE HOME
Created by: Cy DeCosse Incorporated, in cooperation with the Singer Education Department. SINGER is a trademark of The Singer Company and is used under license.

Project Director: Gail Devens
Production Director: Christine Watkins

Editorial Staff: Bernadette Baczynski,
   Paula Brewbaker, Christine Kittleson,
   Bernice Maehren
Art Directors: Nancy McDonough,
   William Nelson
Project Manager: Lucinda Hawker
Writers: Bernadette Baczynski, Betty
   Braden, Gail Devens, Judy Lindahl,
   Barbara Marhoeffer

Director of Photography: Buck Holzemer
Staff Photographers: Jim Brown, Tony Kubat,
   Jerry Robb

Production Staff: Michelle Alexander, Brian
   Berkey, Julie Churchill, Christopher
   Lentz, Douglas Meyers, Nancy Nardone,
   Jean Sherlock, Jennie Smith, Nik Wogstad
Consultants: Depth of Field Fabrics, Bruce
   Dixon, Zoe Graul, Zuelia Ann Hurt, Amy
   Long, Lynn Marquardt, Janet Schneider,
   The Singer Company, Carolyn Thurman,
   Waverly Decorative Fabrics

Sewing Staff: Phyllis Galbraith, Bridget
   Haugh, Julie Huber, Lynn Lohmann,
   Carol Neumann, Kathy Weber

Contributing Manufacturers: Coats & Clark, Inc.;
   Dyno Merchandise Corp.; Fairfield
   Processing Corp.; Marks International, Inc.;
   Risdon Corp.; The Singer Company

Color Separations: La Cromolito
Printing: R. R. Donnelley & Sons Co. (0788)

Fabrics from Waverly Decorative Fabrics,
division of F. Schumacher & Company

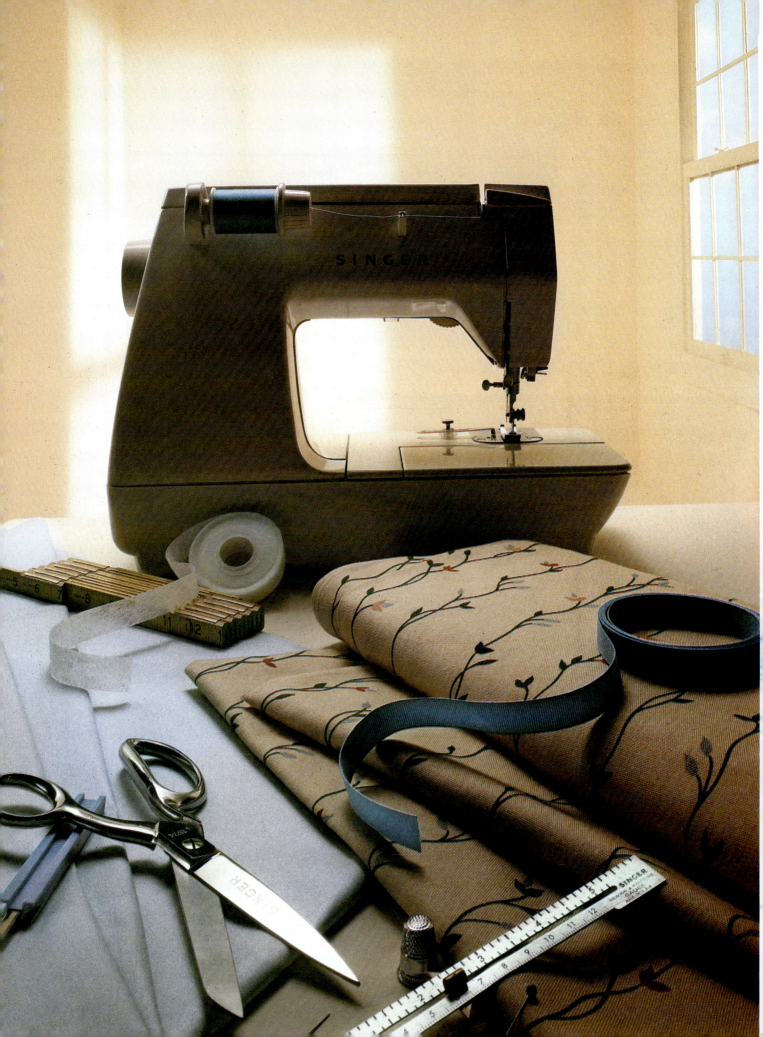

How to Use This Book

Sewing for the Home has a wide selection of decorator home fashions for you to sew. In making these items, we have considered cost, simplicity of construction, ease of care and coordination of colors and patterns. We have also considered the amount of time involved; many of these projects can be completed in an afternoon or evening. Also included are designer customizing hints which you can incorporate into your home decorating projects.

Home Sewing Basics

We start with the basics of fabric and color selection, then show you how to use your sewing machine and its standard equipment to achieve the best sewing results. You will also learn about optional machine attachments that make home decorator sewing faster and easier.

Instructions for many of the projects include alternate sewing methods and suggest timesaving techniques such as fusible web to join two fabrics, fusible backing to stabilize a tieback, or hook and loop tape to close a pillow.

Before you begin to sew, read the information on pages 4 through 21 to acquaint yourself with the basic techniques of home decorator sewing.

Step-by-Step Guidance

This book is divided into four project sections: windows, pillows, tables and beds. For windows, we give instructions for standard favorites such as pinch-pleated draperies and ruffled curtains, along with directions for many other window fashions including five Roman shade variations. Pillows range from simple knife-edge styles to pillows with flanged or shirred edges. For tables, learn how to make a reversible tablecloth, quilted runners, bordered placemats and six different styles of napkins. Make

a bed comforter for your bed or cover an old one, then sew pillow shams and a dust ruffle to match.

At the beginning of each section is an overview of the section. This includes how to take accurate measurements for the projects and what to consider when selecting fabric and sewing aids. Cutting directions are detailed at the beginning of each project. For easy reference, fabrics and notions required to complete the project are included in boxes labeled YOU WILL NEED.

The step-by-step instructions that are given are complete; you do not need to purchase additional patterns. The photographs that accompany the instructions show you how the project should look at each step of its construction.

The sewing techniques you learn for one project can be applied to others. The same method is used for making ruffles on curtains as for pillows or bed accessories. The technique for mitering corners on a tablecloth is the same as on pillows or placemats.

Easy Home Decorator Projects

Experienced sewers can manage any of the projects we have designed; other projects such as knife-edge pillows, shower curtains, napkins or roller shades are suitable for less experienced sewers.

To inspire your creativity and help you visualize finished results, the projects throughout this book are made with coordinating fabrics. You will see how one fabric can be used for many different projects. Start with one project as the focal point of the room, then turn leftover fabrics from larger projects into attractive, coordinating accessories.

We hope the step-by-step guidance, practical shortcuts and designer tips given in *Sewing for the Home* encourage you to design and create your own home decorator fashions.

Fabrics for Home Decorating

Knowledge of fibers, finishes and fabrics will help you select the best fabrics for home sewing. Fiber and finish information is on the bolt-end label or printed on the selvage of decorator fabrics.

Terms to Know

Fiber is the basic unit of yarn before it is made into fabric. Fiber content affects durability and care.

Natural fibers come from nature. They are wool, cotton, silk and linen (flax). Natural fibers are durable, natural insulators.

Man-made fibers are chemically produced. Man-made fibers such as polyester, nylon and acrylic are usually associated with easy-care features and are well suited to home sewing projects.

Blends are combinations of fibers utilizing the best qualities of two or more fibers in one fabric.

A finish is a treatment to a fabric to change its behavior or improve its appearance, care or *hand* (how it feels). Finishes can make a fabric crease-resistant, mildew-resistant, resistant to oil or water-borne stains, or add luster and stability.

A permanent finish is often used to describe crease-resistance and shrinkage-resistance. Few finishes are truly permanent for the life of the fabric. Although they are durable, they may become less effective with laundering and drycleaning.

Decorator fabrics are designed for home decorator projects. They are usually wider than 48" (122 cm) and often have special finishes which are desirable for home items.

Fashion fabrics are used primarily for dressmaker or fashion sewing; however, fabrics such as calico, eyelet, poplin, polished cotton, gingham, sateen and muslin may also be used for the home.

Repeat is the size (length and width) of the pattern or motif printed on the fabric. You will usually need to buy one extra repeat for each length of fabric you use. The size of the repeat is often printed on the label or selvage of decorator fabric.

Selvage is the finished lengthwise edge of a woven fabric.

Grain is the direction in which fabric threads run. Woven fabrics consist of lengthwise threads intersecting crosswise threads. When these threads cross each other at perfect right angles the fabric is *on-grain*. If the intersection of lengthwise and crosswise threads is not at right angles the fabric is *off-grain*. Avoid buying fabric that is printed off-grain; it is difficult to work with and will not hang properly.

Other Practical Considerations

Fabrics should not be prewashed. Many are treated with finishes to protect their beauty and resist soiling. Washing may remove this finish, alter the fabric's hand, or fade the colors. Dryclean your finished projects to keep them looking their best. If you do wash, use cold water and nondetergent soap.

Fabric Selection Guide

Project	Fabric suggestions	Appropriate finishes
Curtains, draperies	Lightweight sheer and semi-sheer fabrics: cotton, cotton-polyester blends, organdy, dotted Swiss, lace, batiste, voile. Mediumweight opaque fabrics such as textured and nubby cotton, linen and blends; open weaves; smooth surfaces such as chintz, polished cotton, antique satin, silk, moire.	Oil and water repellent; sunfast; mildew-resistant; preshrunk so that residual shrinkage will not exceed 1% in either direction.
Shades	For Roman shades and roller shades: closely woven fabrics such as sailcloth, denim, poplin, polished cotton. For bouffant shades: sheers and semi-sheers such as dotted Swiss, eyelet, cotton-polyester blends, chintz, polished cotton.	Oil and water repellent; sunfast; mildew-resistant; preshrunk so that residual shrinkage will not exceed 1% in either direction.
Linings, pillow liners	White or off-white sateen, muslin, sheeting.	Preshrunk linings for washable curtains and draperies.
Pillows, cushions	Closely woven fabrics to retain their shape, such as polished or textured cottons and linens, chintz, velveteen, corduroy.	Oil and water repellent; soil and stain-release.
Tablecloths, napkins placemats	Polished or textured cotton, linen, calico, cotton-polyester blends, quilted fabrics, loosely woven homespun-type cottons.	Oil and water repellent; soil and stain-release; colorfast; easy-care.
Comforters, covers, shams, dust ruffles	Closely-woven, washable fabrics: sheets, brushed cotton flannel, polished cotton, chintz. For ruffles: eyelet, dotted Swiss, lace.	Washable; colorfast; easy-care.

Machine Stitching

Most home decorator sewing can be done entirely by machine with a straight or zigzag stitch. Although machines vary in capabilities, each has the same basic parts and controls. Consult your machine manual to review the threading procedures and to locate the controls that operate the principal parts.

Tension, pressure and stitch length and width are the main adjustments that create perfect straight or zigzag stitching. Choosing the appropriate needle and thread for the sewing project and fabric also helps to create quality stitching.

Tension is the balance between the upper and bobbin threads as they pass through the machine.

When tension is perfectly balanced, the stitches look even on both sides of the fabric because they link midway between fabric layers. Tension that is too tight causes seams to pucker and stitches to break easily. Tension that is too loose results in weak seams.

Pressure regulates the even feeding of fabric layers. When pressure is too heavy, the bottom fabric layer gathers, forcing the upper layer ahead of the presser foot. This unevenness can make a difference of several inches at the end of a long seam, such as one on a curtain. Pressure that is too light may cause skipped stitches, crooked stitching lines and weak, loose stitches.

Fabrics for Home Decorating

Knowledge of fibers, finishes and fabrics will help you select the best fabrics for home sewing. Fiber and finish information is on the bolt-end label or printed on the selvage of decorator fabrics.

Terms to Know

Fiber is the basic unit of yarn before it is made into fabric. Fiber content affects durability and care.

Natural fibers come from nature. They are wool, cotton, silk and linen (flax). Natural fibers are durable, natural insulators.

Man-made fibers are chemically produced. Man-made fibers such as polyester, nylon and acrylic are usually associated with easy-care features and are well suited to home sewing projects.

Blends are combinations of fibers utilizing the best qualities of two or more fibers in one fabric.

A finish is a treatment to a fabric to change its behavior or improve its appearance, care or *hand* (how it feels). Finishes can make a fabric crease-resistant, mildew-resistant, resistant to oil or water-borne stains, or add luster and stability.

A permanent finish is often used to describe crease-resistance and shrinkage-resistance. Few finishes are truly permanent for the life of the fabric. Although they are durable, they may become less effective with laundering and drycleaning.

Decorator fabrics are designed for home decorator projects. They are usually wider than 48" (122 cm) and often have special finishes which are desirable for home items.

Fashion fabrics are used primarily for dressmaker or fashion sewing; however, fabrics such as calico, eyelet, poplin, polished cotton, gingham, sateen and muslin may also be used for the home.

Repeat is the size (length and width) of the pattern or motif printed on the fabric. You will usually need to buy one extra repeat for each length of fabric you use. The size of the repeat is often printed on the label or selvage of decorator fabric.

Selvage is the finished lengthwise edge of a woven fabric.

Grain is the direction in which fabric threads run. Woven fabrics consist of lengthwise threads intersecting crosswise threads. When these threads cross each other at perfect right angles the fabric is *on-grain*. If the intersection of lengthwise and crosswise threads is not at right angles the fabric is *off-grain*. Avoid buying fabric that is printed off-grain; it is difficult to work with and will not hang properly.

Other Practical Considerations

Fabrics should not be prewashed. Many are treated with finishes to protect their beauty and resist soiling. Washing may remove this finish, alter the fabric's hand, or fade the colors. Dryclean your finished projects to keep them looking their best. If you do wash, use cold water and nondetergent soap.

Fabric Selection Guide

Project	Fabric suggestions	Appropriate finishes
Curtains, draperies	Lightweight sheer and semi-sheer fabrics: cotton, cotton-polyester blends, organdy, dotted Swiss, lace, batiste, voile. Mediumweight opaque fabrics such as textured and nubby cotton, linen and blends; open weaves; smooth surfaces such as chintz, polished cotton, antique satin, silk, moire.	Oil and water repellent; sunfast; mildew-resistant; preshrunk so that residual shrinkage will not exceed 1% in either direction.
Shades	For Roman shades and roller shades: closely woven fabrics such as sailcloth, denim, poplin, polished cotton. For bouffant shades: sheers and semi-sheers such as dotted Swiss, eyelet, cotton-polyester blends, chintz, polished cotton.	Oil and water repellent; sunfast; mildew-resistant; preshrunk so that residual shrinkage will not exceed 1% in either direction.
Linings, pillow liners	White or off-white sateen, muslin, sheeting.	Preshrunk linings for washable curtains and draperies.
Pillows, cushions	Closely woven fabrics to retain their shape, such as polished or textured cottons and linens, chintz, velveteen, corduroy.	Oil and water repellent; soil and stain-release.
Tablecloths, napkins placemats	Polished or textured cotton, linen, calico, cotton-polyester blends, quilted fabrics, loosely woven homespun-type cottons.	Oil and water repellent; soil and stain-release; colorfast; easy-care.
Comforters, covers, shams, dust ruffles	Closely-woven, washable fabrics: sheets, brushed cotton flannel, polished cotton, chintz. For ruffles: eyelet, dotted Swiss, lace.	Washable; colorfast; easy-care.

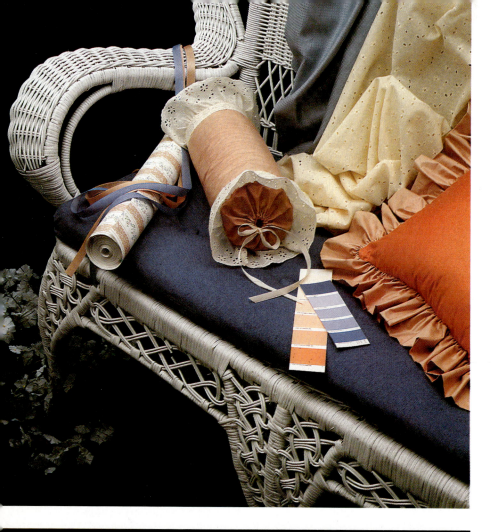

Mixing & Matching Fabrics

Using a number of complementary patterns and colors helps to connect areas in rooms and give your home continuity.

Geometric prints, stripes, patterns and solids can work together to give a room style and interest. Fabric manufacturers make it easy to coordinate fabrics by designing groups of complementary patterns, prints and solids which you can use in any combination.

If you coordinate fabrics on your own, unroll the bolts and compare them side-by-side in natural light. Examine the fabrics from several angles to judge the compatibility of print and color.

Bolts often come from different dye lots. To avoid problems of slight color variations or differences in pattern printing, buy fabrics for large projects from only one bolt. Check patterned fabrics to be sure they are printed on the straight grain. Also remember that wider fabrics generally mean fewer seams, especially in curtains.

Consider where the fabric will be used and how it relates to other fabrics in the room. Most stores have display cuts or swatch books of their decorator fabrics available. They may permit you to take swatches home. This gives you a chance to see the fabric next to other fabrics and lets you see it in your home lighting which may be very different from store lighting. If swatches are not available, ask for a sample from the bolt or buy a small piece before you invest in a large cut.

Choosing Colors

Keep these points in mind as you shop for fabrics.

• What colors already exist in the room? Take paint chips, carpet swatches or small cushions with you when you compare fabric.

• What wood tones are in your room? Fabric colors can enhance the natural tones and richness of wood.

• Color affects your mood. Pastels, neutrals and cooler shades, such as blues and some greens, are soothing. Bright shades and warmer colors like reds and yellows tend to stimulate. Dark colors create a cozy feeling.

• Color alters perceptions. Colors appear darker against light backgrounds, lighter against dark surfaces. Warm colors make objects seem larger, while cool colors make them recede. In general, avoid using bold contrasting colors in small rooms.

• Keep the room's exposure in mind. You may want to warm a northern exposure with warm tones, or cool down a hot sunny room with pale blues.

• Light colors show soil more readily than dark colors.

• At windows, pale colors diffuse light while dark colors block it. Hold up a length of fabric in direct sunlight to see if it creates the effect you want.

• Finally, consider your own preferences. Use these guidelines and your own taste to choose colors and patterns that beautify your home and reflect your personal style.

Equipment & Notions

The Basics

Home decorator sewing requires the same basic equipment as dressmaker sewing, with the addition of tools for measuring windows and furniture. Using the proper equipment makes the work easier and the results more satisfying.

1) Needle threader eases threading of hand and machine needles.

2) Pins with plastic or glass heads are easier to see and handle.

3) Thimble protects your middle finger when you sew by hand.

4) Needles for general hand sewing are *sharps*. Buy a package of assorted sizes for various sewing tasks.

5) T-pins are long, sturdy, broad-headed pins which are used to anchor fabrics to solid surfaces.

6) Quilting pins are extra long and useful for working with heavy or thick materials.

7) All-purpose thread is used for hand and machine sewing on most fabrics. Choose all-cotton, cotton-wrapped polyester or all-polyester thread, depending on the fiber content of the fabric.

Measuring Tools

The most important consideration in home decorator sewing is accurate measuring. The following measuring aids help you make correct calculations for buying and cutting fabric.

1) Carpenter's square is an L-shaped ruler, used to determine the perfect right angles and square corners that are essential to the fit of curtains, shades, tablecloths and pillows.

2) Wood folding ruler is used for measuring large areas. Because of its stability, this ruler is more accurate than a tape measure.

3) Yardstick is used for measuring long, flat lengths of fabric, and for marking and squaring grain lines. The surface of the yardstick should be smooth so it does not snag fabric.

4) Spring-return metal tape measures windows and other large areas. It is also handy for measuring around curves.

5) Seam gauge makes quick, short measurements such as those for hems. The 6" (15 cm) metal or plastic ruler has a sliding marker for accuracy in measuring.

Marking & Cutting Tools

After making careful calculations and taking accurate measurements, mark and cut the fabric in preparation for sewing. Have on hand an assortment of marking tools for various fabric colors and textures. Good quality cutting tools are also a smart investment.

1) Cutting board is marked with horizontal and vertical lines, and is useful for laying out and cutting lengths of fabric up to 2 yards (1.85 meters). It is made of heavy cardboard so fabric can be pinned in place. Two boards may be necessary for large items such as floor-length curtains.

2) Tailor's chalk is specially designed to mark directly on fabric and rub off easily.

3) Trimmers have straight handles and are used for trimming and straightening edges. A lightweight, slim blade aids accuracy.

4) Seam ripper is used to remove stitches. Use it with care to avoid ripping fabric.

5) Bent-handled shears allow fabric to remain flat during cutting. Shears should be lightweight, easy to handle and 8" or 9" (20.5 or 23 cm) long.

6) Liquid marking pencils make sharp, defined lines on firm fabrics. One type of pencil makes a mark that can be removed with clear water; the other makes a mark that disappears in 48 hours. Test marking pencils on a fabric scrap before using. Ironing permanently sets the markings; if markings are on the right side of the fabric, do not press until they are removed.

Notions

Notions serve three purposes in home decorator sewing. Some, such as the rings used on Roman shades, are essential to the construction of an item; others, such as fusible web and fabric glue, make sewing easier. Notions such as braids, trims, pipings and ribbons are simply decorative.

1) Decorative trims such as bias tape **(1a)**, piping **(1b)** and ribbon **(1c)** are available in a wide range of colors and styles to complement the items you sew. Select trims with the same care requirements as the decorator fabric.

2) Cords, tapes and rings (2a) have specific uses on certain projects. These notions are described in the directions for projects which require them.

3) Fusible web is used for hemming or for bonding two layers of fabric together. It is available in narrow strips for hems, or in 18" (46 cm) widths for fusing larger areas.

4) Fabric adhesives such as glue stick **(4a)** and craft or white glue **(4b)** may be used for temporary basting, or for permanently applying batting or trims to items which will not receive much handling.

5) Liquid fray preventer dries invisibly and prevents the raw edge of fabric from fraying. Use it as a temporary agent to prevent raveling while working with fabric, or as a permanent finish on exposed seams and edges.

6) Stain-resistant spray can be used on many home decorating items to prevent spills from soaking into fabric. To apply, follow instructions on the container.

Machine Stitching

Most home decorator sewing can be done entirely by machine with a straight or zigzag stitch. Although machines vary in capabilities, each has the same basic parts and controls. Consult your machine manual to review the threading procedures and to locate the controls that operate the principal parts.

Tension, pressure and stitch length and width are the main adjustments that create perfect straight or zigzag stitching. Choosing the appropriate needle and thread for the sewing project and fabric also helps to create quality stitching.

Tension is the balance between the upper and bobbin threads as they pass through the machine.

When tension is perfectly balanced, the stitches look even on both sides of the fabric because they link midway between fabric layers. Tension that is too tight causes seams to pucker and stitches to break easily. Tension that is too loose results in weak seams.

Pressure regulates the even feeding of fabric layers. When pressure is too heavy, the bottom fabric layer gathers, forcing the upper layer ahead of the presser foot. This unevenness can make a difference of several inches at the end of a long seam, such as one on a curtain. Pressure that is too light may cause skipped stitches, crooked stitching lines and weak, loose stitches.

Stitch length is controlled with a regulator that is on an inch scale from 0 to 20, a metric scale from 0 to 4, or a numerical scale from 0 to 9. On the metric and numerical scales, higher numbers form a longer stitch, lower numbers a shorter stitch. For normal stitching, set the regulator at 10 to 12 stitches per inch (2.5 cm). This setting is equivalent to 2.5 to 3 on the metric scale, and 5 on the numerical scale.

Needle, size 14/80, is used for general-purpose sewing on mediumweight fabrics. Because the firm weave and glazed finish of many home decorator fabrics dull a needle quickly, change the needle often. A bent, blunt or burred needle damages fabric. Prevent damage to the needle by removing pins from the seam as you come to them. Never sew over pins or let them get under the fabric where they may come in contact with the feed dogs.

Thread for general-purpose sewing is suitable for most home decorator projects. Use an all-purpose weight. Choose all-cotton, all-polyester, or cotton-wrapped polyester thread that matches the fiber content of the fabric. For balanced tension, use the same type of thread in the bobbin and the needle.

Thread the machine correctly; incorrect threading can cause a stitch to be too loose or too tight. To rethread the machine, remove the spool completely and begin again, in case the thread has tangled in the tension or over the spool pin.

Use a scrap of fabric to test the tension, pressure and stitch length before starting to sew. To check the balance of the tension, you may want to thread the machine with different colors for upper and bobbin threads so the stitches are easier to see.

Perfect Straight & Zigzag Stitching

Straight stitches should link midway between fabric layers so stitches are the same length on both sides of fabric. Adjust tension and pressure so stitches do not break easily and the seam does not pucker.

Zigzag stitching is adjusted correctly when the links interlock at the corner of each stitch. Stitches should lie flat. Adjust the zigzag width and density with the stitch length and width regulators.

Machine Stitching Terms

Bastestitching (a) is the longest straight stitch on the machine: 6 on the inch scale, 4 on the metric scale, and 9 on the numerical scale. Some sewing machines have a separate built-in bastestitch **(b)** that makes two stitches to the inch (2.5 cm). Use it for speed-basting straight seams.

Gathering stitch is done with two rows of bastestitching placed ½" (1.3 cm) and ¼" (6 mm) from the fabric edge. Loosen tension, use heavier bobbin thread, and pull up bobbin thread to form gathers **(a)**. For long areas of gathers, zigzag over cord, string or dental floss without catching cord in the stitch **(b)**. Pull up cord to gather.

Edgestitching is placed on the edge of a hem or fold. The straight-stitch foot and straight-stitch needle plate aid in the close control needed for this stitching. The narrow foot rides on the folded edge, and the small hole of the needle plate keeps fragile fabric from being drawn into the feed dogs.

Basic Seams

All seams in home decorator sewing are ½" (1.3 cm) unless otherwise specified. To secure straight seams, backstitch at each end of the seam by stitching in reverse for ½" (1.3 cm). Four seam techniques are used in home decorator sewing.

1) Plain seam is suitable for almost every fabric and sewing application when you plan to enclose the seam or cover it with a lining.

2) French seam eliminates raw edges in exposed seams. In dressmaking, the French seam is used primarily on sheer fabrics; in home decorating use it whenever a seam is visible on the wrong side or is subjected to frequent laundering.

3) Interlocking fell or self-bound seam, like the French seam, completely encloses raw edges. For this seam, sew on the wrong side of the fabric. Use the narrow hemmer attachment as a timesaver.

4) Overedge or zigzag seams are plain seams with a zigzag finish to prevent raveling. Use them on heavy, textured fabrics that are too bulky for French or self-bound seams. Some machines have overedge settings that stitch and finish the edge in one step. For this seam, allow ¼" (6 mm) seam allowances.

Long straight seams tend to pucker in some fabrics, especially sheers. To prevent this, practice taut sewing. As you sew, pull equally on the fabric in front and back of the needle as if the fabric were in an embroidery hoop. Do not stretch. Pull the fabric taut, and let it feed through the machine on its own.

How to Sew a Plain Seam

1) Pin right sides of fabric together, placing pins at right angles to seam line for easy removal. If using basting tape, place it at the raw edge and do not stitch through it.

2) Use seam guide to sew even seams. Backstitch to secure; then stitch seam, removing pins as you come to them. Backstitch at end of seam. Lift presser foot and remove fabric by pulling 2" to 3" (5 to 7.5 cm) of thread to the left.

3) Clip threads close to the end of seam. Press seam open or to one side. If seam is on the selvage, clip selvage diagonally every 1" to 6" (2.5 to 15 cm) to prevent the seam from puckering.

How to Sew a French Seam

1) Pin fabric *wrong* sides together. Stitch a scant ¼" (6 mm) seam. Press seam allowance to one side. For narrower finished seam, trim seam allowance to ⅛" (3 mm).

2) Turn fabric panels right sides together to enclose the trimmed seam allowance. Stitching line should be exactly on fold.

3) Stitch ⅜" (1 cm) from folded edge, enclosing first seam. Press the seam to one side. If first seam was trimmed, stitch ¼" (6 mm) from the edge.

How to Sew an Interlocking Fell Seam

1) Pin fabric, right sides together, with edge of top layer ½" (1.3 cm) from edge of bottom layer. Stitch ¾" (2 cm) from edge of bottom fabric layer.

2) Fold and press ¼" (6 mm) on seam allowance of bottom layer so that it meets edge of top layer. Fold and press again, covering the stitching line.

3) Edgestitch close to fold. Press seam to one side, holding fabric taut to eliminate puckering. Or use narrow hemmer for final stitching (page 18).

Three Ways to Sew an Overedge Seam

Zigzag plain seam. Stitch ½" (1.3 cm) plain seam. Zigzag seam allowances together close to raw edge. This eliminates trimming the seam, but results in a wider seam. Press seam to one side. This is the easiest overedge seam to sew and is suitable for most fabrics.

Zigzag narrow seam. Stitch ½" (1.3 cm) plain seam. Zigzag seam allowances together, stitching with wide zigzag close to stitching. Trim seam allowances close to zigzag stitching. This seam requires time for trimming. It can be used as an alternative to French seams.

Overedge seam. Trim seams to ¼" (6 mm) before stitching. Then stitch seam with built-in overedge stitch. This makes a straight seam and zigzags over cut edge in one step. Use this seam on medium to heavyweight fabrics which ravel.

Timesaving Accessories

Many home decorator sewing projects require long seams or hems. There are several machine attachments and special feet that speed hemming, binding, ruffling and straight stitching. Some of these accessories come with the machine; others are available from your machine dealer.

Before buying special-purpose attachments, find out if your machine has a high, low or slanted shank. Consult the machine manual if you are not sure what type of shank your machine has. Snap-on presser feet will fit any machine with a snap-on, all-purpose shank.

Special-purpose foot is used for decorative stitching and machine embroidery. The plastic foot lets you see the stitching easily, and a groove under the foot allows for a build-up of thread. Use the foot for general-purpose sewing and special tasks such as closely-spaced zigzag overedge.

Zipper and cording foot is used for inserting zippers, applying snap tape and for making and applying cording. It adjusts to either side of the needle, allowing stitching to be placed close to bulk on one side of the seam.

Even Feed™ **foot** feeds top and bottom layers of fabric at the same rate, ensuring that seams start and end evenly. This foot helps keep plaids and other matched designs aligned in long seams. Use on heavy, bulky or quilted fabrics, as with insulated shades.

Narrow hemmer automatically double-folds the fabric edge and stitches a ⅛" (3 mm) hem without pressing or pinning. The foot is useful for hemming and for stitching interlocking fell seams.

Seam guide helps keep seam allowances even. It attaches to the bed of the machine (**a**) and adjusts for seam widths up to 1¼" (3.2 cm). A magnetic seam guide (**b**) attaches to any metal machine bed.

Quilter guide-bar rides in the first row of stitching to form perfectly parallel quilting lines. Use it for topstitching or channel quilting. The bar adjusts to widths up to 3" (7.5 cm) and can be used on either side of the needle.

Ruffler Attachment

Ruffler attachment automatically gathers strips of light or mediumweight fabric. Stitch length affects fullness; short stitches give more fullness and longer stitches give less. Gather one layer of fabric (**a**).

Or gather one layer and attach it to another layer of fabric in one step (**b**). Insert fullness at every stitch, or at 6 or 12-stitch intervals. Use this attachment for ruffles on curtains, pillows or dust ruffles.

Blindstitch Hem Foot & Guide

Blindstitch hem foot is used with the built-in blind hemming stitch. The foot (**a**) positions the hem for sewing with straight and zigzag stitches which are

barely visible on the right side. Blindstitch hem guide (**b**) is used with the general-purpose foot to position the hem for blindstitching.

Binder Attachment

Binder attachment is used to fold and attach bias bindings in one step. First, cut a sharp point at end of bias strip. Feed the point through scroll on foot (**a**). Pull point through

so strip folds to the inside. Sew a few stitches to hold bias fold in place. Insert fabric to be bound into slot between scroll edges (**b**). Adjust position of foot so that

needle stitches on edge of fold (**c**). Guide fabric gently as you stitch. Use the binder attachment for finishing edges of any fabric.

Hand Stitching

Almost all sewing for home decorator projects can be done on the machine, but sometimes hand stitching is necessary. Closing seam openings on pillows, attaching trims and finishing hems are tasks which may require delicate hand sewing.

To make hand stitching easier, run the thread through beeswax to make it stronger and prevent it from snarling. Use a long needle for the running stitch. Hemming and tacking are usually easier with a short needle.

Running stitch is a straight stitch used for temporary basting, easing, gathering or stitching seams. Work from right to left, taking several stitches onto needle before pulling it through. For easing or gathering or for seams, make stitches ⅛" to ¼" (3 to 6 mm) long. For basting, make stitches ½" to ¾" (1.3 to 2 cm) long; use longer stitches for speed-basting.

Slipstitch is a nearly invisible stitch for hems, seam openings, linings or trims. Work from right to left, holding folded edge in left hand. Bring needle up through fold and pull thread through. Then take a tiny stitch in body of fabric, directly opposite point where thread came out. Continue taking stitches every ¼" (6 mm).

Blindstitch makes a hem that is inconspicuous from either side. Work from right to left with needle pointing left. Take a tiny stitch in body of fabric. Roll hem edge back slightly and take next stitch in underside of hem, ¼" to ½" (6 mm to 1.3 cm) to left of first stitch. Do not pull thread too tightly.

Tacking is used to attach rings and weights, secure linings or hold facings in place. Using double thread, take two or three stitches in the same place, one on top of the other. Secure with a backstitch. When tacking through more than one layer of fabric, do not sew through to outside layer.

Padded Work Surface

Make a padded work surface to lay out an entire panel for cutting, measuring, squaring off ends and pressing. The square corners and ample width make it easier to work with square and rectangular shapes. Fabric does not slide on the muslin-covered surface; you can also pin into it and press directly on it.

For small projects, use the *square* end of a regular ironing board as a work surface.

Use a steam-spray iron for all your pressing needs. To press fabric, lift and lower the iron in one place. This up-and-down motion prevents fabrics from stretching or distorting. Let the steam do the work. To make sharp creases or to smooth a stubborn wrinkle, spray the fabric with water or spray sizing.

YOU WILL NEED

Hollow door or ¾" (2 cm) plywood, approximately 3' × 7' (.95 × 2.16 m), set on saw horses.

Padding, cotton batting (not polyester), table pads or blankets, ¼" to ½" (6 mm to 1.3 cm) thick, enough to overlap door or plywood 6" (15 cm) on all sides.

Muslin or unpatterned sheet, approximately 6" (15 cm) larger than door or plywood on all sides.

How to Make a Padded Work Surface

1) Place layers of padding on the floor or on a large, flat surface. Center the door on top of the padding; cut padding 6" (15 cm) larger than the door on all sides.

2) Fold padding over one long edge of the door and tack with 4 or 5 staples. Pull padding on opposite edge and tack. Repeat on both ends. Secure with staples 3" (7.5 cm) apart.

3) Center padded door on top of muslin. Wrap and fasten with staples 3" (7.5 cm) apart. Turn right side up and spray muslin with water. As it dries, muslin shrinks slightly so cover fits tightly.

Curtains

Curtains are a traditional favorite for window fashions. They are flat, nonpleated panels, so they are easier to clean and press than many other window treatments.

Curtains are often made of lightweight or sheer fabrics. Heavier fabrics such as linen, chintz, or textured or polished cotton look best for formal, floor-length curtains. Lighter, crisper fabrics work well for casual, sill-length and cafe curtains. Sheer curtains are usually two and one-half to three times the fullness of the finished width; heavier fabrics require only double fullness.

Mount curtains at windows on stationary rods or poles. Rods may be plain, covered with shirred fabric between the curtain panels, or wide and flat such as Continental™ and cornice rods.

Casings, also known as rod pockets, are hems stitched in place along the upper edge of curtains. The hems are open at both ends so a curtain rod or pole can be inserted.

Headings are optional on curtains. The heading creates a decorative ruffle above the casing along the upper edge of the curtain.

Linings add weight and body to curtains. Although a lining may not be necessary, it can improve a curtain's appearance and give it a custom look.

Tab top curtains have fabric loops instead of a casing along the upper edge. These curtains are used with decorative brass or wooden poles.

Ruffled curtains have a graceful appearance. Ruffles add weight to curtains and make them hang and drape more attractively.

Tiebacks are separate fabric strips which hold curtains open and emphasize the drape of the curtain. Tiebacks can be straight, shaped or ruffled and are usually stationary on panel curtains.

Shower curtains are flat, one-piece, hemmed curtains with evenly-spaced holes along the upper edge for hanging with hooks or rings.

Casing Styles for Curtains

Simple casing is stitched along the upper edge of the curtain. It may be used for sheer curtains that hang behind draperies, a valance or cornice.

Heading creates a ruffled edge above casing. Headings are from 1" to 5" (2.5 to 12.5 cm) deep, depending on curtain length and weight of the fabric.

Wide casing and heading are used with a Continental or cornice rod. They are well suited for floor-length curtains, where casing and heading depth should balance with curtain length.

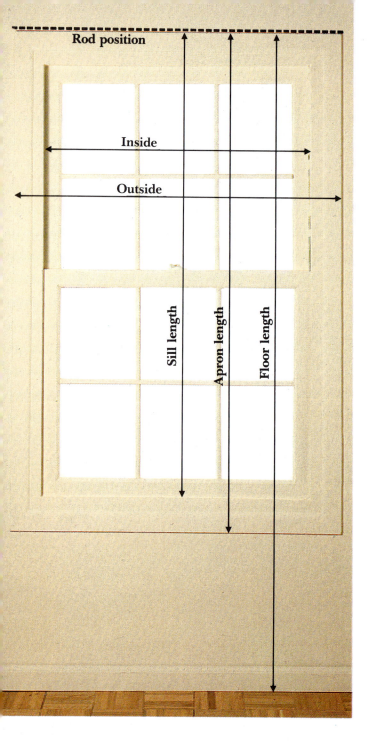

Rod position

Inside

Outside

Sill length

Apron length

Floor length

Measuring the Window

Before measuring windows, select the style of curtain, drapery or shade you will make. The style of window treatment determines what installation hardware is necessary. Next, decide exactly where the window treatment will be placed; install the hardware and measure this area for the finished size of the curtain, shade or drapery.

Curtain rods may be attached to the window frame, within or at the sides of the frame, on the wall above the frame, or at the ceiling.

Mounting boards are necessary for hanging Roman shades and other shades based on the Roman shade construction. These 1" × 2" (2.5 × 5 cm) boards are cut to the width of the shade, stapled or tacked to the shade's upper edge, then installed at the window. An *inside mounted* shade fits firmly inside the top of the window frame. An *outside mounted* shade is installed on the wall above the frame. A *hybrid mounted* shade is a combination mount. The mounting board is placed inside the window, but the shade extends over part of the window frame.

Roller shades are installed inside or on the window frame, or on the wall above.

Follow these guidelines for accurate measuring:

1) Use a folding ruler or metal tape for measuring; cloth tapes may stretch or sag.

2) Measure and record the measurements for all windows separately, even if they *appear* to be the same size. Size differences, even if slight, should be taken into account when constructing window treatments.

3) When measuring for a shade that fits inside the window, measure the window width at the top, center and bottom to determine if it is true and square.

4) When measuring for curtains on a window without an apron, measure to at least 4" (10 cm) below the sill.

Window Measurements for Curtains, Shades and Draperies

Treatment	Finished Length	Finished Width
Curtains	Measure from top of rod or heading to desired length (sill, apron or floor).	Measure rod from end to end, plus *returns* (short ends of the rod that stand out from the wall).
Roller Shades	Measure from top of roller to sill.	Measure length of roller.
Other Shades	Measure from top of mounting board to sill or desired length.	Measure mounting board from end to end.
Shower Curtain	Measure from bottom of rod to desired length.	Measure length of rod.
Use these measurements with chart (page 27) to estimate amount of fabric needed.		

Estimating Yardage

Because fabric widths vary, yardage cannot be figured until the fabric has been selected. After you have taken the necessary measurements and determined the finished size of the curtain, shade or drapery, you must add to the length and width for seams, hems, headings and fullness. This is the *cut length*. Use the cut length to estimate the amount of fabric you will need. For curtains and draperies, use the amounts as listed below and transfer the correct amount to the chart (right). For shade yardage, see individual instructions for each type of shade.

Determining Length

To the *finished length*, add the amount needed for lower hems, casings, headings and pattern repeat.

Lower hems. Add double the desired hem to the finished length. For mediumweight fabrics, use a 4" (10 cm) double-fold hem on floor-length curtains or draperies; add 8" (20.5 cm) to the length. Or on short curtains or valances, use a 1" to 3" (2.5 to 7.5 cm) double-fold hem; add 2" to 6" (5 to 15 cm) to the length. For sheer and lightweight fabrics, a deeper double-fold hem of 5" to 6" (12.5 to 15 cm) may be used; add 10" to 12" (25.5 to 30.5 cm) to the length.

Casings and headings. For simple casings with no heading, add an amount equal to the diameter of the rod plus ½" (1.3 cm) to turn under and ¼" to 1" (6 mm to 2.5 cm) ease. The amount of ease depends on the size of the rod and thickness of the fabric. Lightweight fabrics require less ease; casings for large rods require more. For casings with headings, use the formula for a simple casing, adding to it an amount twice the depth of the heading.

Pattern repeat. Fabrics with patterns (motifs) need to be matched. Measure the distance between motifs and add that amount to the length of each panel.

Determining Width

To the *finished width*, add the amount needed for seams, side hems and fullness.

Seams. For multi-width panels, add 1" (2.5 cm) for each seam. Panels that are not wider than the fabric do not require an extra amount for seams.

Side hems. Add 4" (10 cm) per panel for à 1" (2.5 cm) double-fold hem on each side of the panel.

Fullness. Fabric weight determines fullness. For medium to heavyweight fabrics, add two to two and one-half times the finished width of the curtain. For sheer and lightweight fabrics, add two and one-half to three times the finished width.

Make a copy of this chart and fill it in to help you figure the correct amount of fabric needed for curtains, shades or draperies.

Figuring Yardage

Cut Length	in. (cm)
For fabrics *not* requiring pattern match:	
1) Finished length	
2) Bottom hem (double for most fabrics)	+
3) Casing/heading	+
4) Cut length for each width or part width	=
For fabrics requiring pattern match:	
1) Cut length (figure as above)	
2) Size of pattern repeat (distance between motifs)	÷
3) Number of repeats needed*	=
4) Cut length for each width or part width: multiply size of repeat by number of repeats needed	

Cut Width	
1) Finished width	
2) Fullness (how many times the finished width)	×
3) Width times fullness	=
4) Side hems	+
5) Total width needed	=
6) Width of fabric	
7) Number of fabric widths: total width needed divided by width of fabric*	

Total Fabric Needed	
1) Cut length (as figured above)	
2) Number of fabric widths (as figured above)	×
3) Total fabric length	=
4) Number of yds. (meters) needed: total fabric length divided by 36" (100 cm)	yds. (m)

*Round up to the nearest whole number.

NOTE: Add extra fabric for straightening ends.

NOTE: Half of the width (determined above) will be used for each curtain panel. To piece panels, adjust width measurement to include 1" (2.5 cm) for each seam.

Cutting & Matching

Cut fabric on the true lengthwise and crosswise grain to *square* the ends. Squaring ensures that curtains will always hang straight. Most fabrics should be squared by pulling a thread on the crosswise grain and cutting along the thread.

Avoid prints that are obviously off-grain. If these fabrics are cut on-grain, the design motif will be crooked and impossible to match at seams and edges. Many prints and woven patterns are only slightly off-grain, but their unevenness may be more apparent once the curtains are hung. Square the ends of these fabrics by cutting on a line of the design rather than on the crosswise grain.

Most decorator fabrics have a permanent finish which holds the threads in place. Chintz, polished cotton and other permanent-finish fabrics can be squared by simply cutting straight across the ends.

To obtain the desired finished curtain width, you may need to seam several widths of fabric together. Match the design motif of the fabric carefully so that seams are as inconspicuous as possible.

Three Ways to Straighten Crosswise Ends

Pull one or two threads across the width of the fabric, from selvage to selvage. Cut on the line that appears after threads have been pulled out.

Use a carpenter's square to straighten fabrics that have a permanent finish. Place one side of square parallel to selvage. Mark along other side of square; cut on marked line. Or align selvage with corner of table; cut across end.

Locate a design that runs straight across the fabric on the crosswise grain. Cut along the design. Consider depth of hem or heading when determining placement of the design on the finished curtain.

Tips for Matching Design Motifs

Match motifs at the selvage when using decorator fabrics. Motifs on these fabrics are split evenly at the selvage (a) for matching widths easily. Press under one selvage and lap it over the matching motif (b). Stitch seam.

Use fusible web to align motifs for stitching. Press under one seam allowance. Place fusing strips on opposite seam allowance. Match design from right side and press lightly with dry iron. Turn fused seam to wrong side and stitch.

Match motifs from wrong side by placing point of pin through matching design details. Pin at close intervals to prevent shifting. Stitch using Even Feed™ foot to keep seam aligned, removing pins as you come to them.

Hemming

If you have measured, figured and cut accurately, your curtains should fit windows perfectly once they are hemmed. For the neatest and easiest hems, follow the procedure used in professional workrooms: sew the lower hems first, the side hems next, and casings and headings last.

Side and lower hems of unlined curtains are almost always double to provide strength, weight and stability. The easiest way to make a double-fold hem is to press it in place on an ironing board or padded work surface. Use a seam gauge to measure each fold. As you make the fold, pin the fabric to the padding, placing the pins so they do not interfere with pressing. If side edges are on the selvage, cut off selvage or clip it every 1" to 6" (2.5 to 15 cm).

Curtains hang better when hems are weighted or anchored. Sew small weights into the hems at the lower corners and bottoms of seams to keep the curtain from pulling or puckering. Use heavier weights for full-length curtains, lighter weights for lightweight fabrics and shorter curtains.

How to Sew Double-fold Hems

1) Turn a scant 3" (7.5 cm) to wrong side on lower edge of curtain. Pin along cut edge. Press fold. Turn under another 3" (7.5 cm), pin and press in place. Finish lower hem using one of the methods below.

2) Turn a scant 1" (2.5 cm) to the wrong side for side hems. Pin and press. Fold under another 1" (2.5 cm); pin and press. Tack weights inside the second fold at side corners, if desired.

3) Press the side hems in place. When the hems have been pressed, finish them with straight stitching, machine blindstitching or fusible web.

Three Ways to Finish Curtain Hems

Straight-stitch on folded hem edge, using 8 to 10 stitches per inch (2.5 cm). When stitching three layers of fabric, lessen pressure slightly and stitch slowly.

Machine blindstitch to make stitches almost invisible on right side. After pressing, fold hem back to right side, leaving a fold of fabric 1/8" (3 mm) from hem edge. Set machine to blindstitch. Adjust zigzag stitch to take tiny bite into curtain only.

Fuse hem in place. Tuck strip of fusible web between pressed hem and curtain. Follow manufacturer's instructions for fusing, using damp press cloth for additional steam. Most fusibles require 15 seconds for permanent bonding.

Casings & Headings

A casing or *rod pocket* is the hem along the upper edge of the curtain or valance. The curtain rod is inserted through the casing so that the fullness of the curtain falls into soft gathers.

Before cutting the curtains, decide on the casing style. A simple casing places the curtain rod at the uppermost edge of the curtain.

For simple casings, add to the cut length an amount equal to the diameter of the rod plus ½" (1.3 cm) to turn under and ¼" to 1" (6 mm to 2.5 cm) ease. The amount of ease depends on the size of the rod and thickness of the fabric.

A heading is a gathered edge above the casing. It finishes the curtain more decoratively than a simple casing. Curtains with headings do not require cornices or valances.

For casings with headings, use the formula for a simple casing, adding to it an amount twice the depth of the heading. Headings may be from 1" to 5" (2.5 to 12.5 cm) deep. The depth of the heading

must be determined before the curtains are cut. The heading depth should be appropriate for the length of the curtain: in general, the longer the curtain, the deeper the heading.

Wooden, brass or plastic poles may be covered with a *shirred pole cover*. The exposed pole between the curtain panels is covered with a casing made from a shirred tube of matching fabric (above). The casing may be plain or have a heading the same height as the curtain heading. Wide poles and casings are more than decorative. They often are used to conceal a shade heading, the plain heading on shirred curtains, or the traverse rod of sheer or lightweight curtains.

Wide casings are used on the flat *Continental™ rod* or *cornice rod*. These rods are 4½" (11.5 cm) wide. A cornice rod is actually two regular curtain rods attached with a spacer between them.

Finish lower and side hems of curtains before sewing casings and headings.

How to Sew a Simple Casing

1) Determine casing depth by loosely pinning a curtain fabric strip around the rod. Remove rod and measure the distance from the top of the strip to the pin. Add ½" (1.3 cm) to be turned under.

2) Press under ½" (1.3 cm) along upper cut edge of curtain panel. Fold over again and press to form a hem equal to amount measured in step 1.

3) Stitch close to folded hem edge to form casing, backstitching at both ends. If desired, stitch again close to the upper edge to create a sharp crease appropriate for flat or oval curtain rods.

How to Sew a Casing with a Heading

1) Determine the depth of the casing as directed in step 1, above. Determine the depth of heading, opposite. Press under ½" (1.3 cm) along upper cut edge of the curtain panel. Fold and press again to form hem equal to casing plus heading depth.

2) Stitch close to folded edge, backstitching at both ends. Mark heading depth with a pin at each end of panel. Stitch again at marked depth. To aid straight stitching, apply a strip of masking tape to the bed of the machine at heading depth, or use seam guide.

3) Insert rod through casing and gather curtain evenly onto rod. Adjust heading by pulling up the folded edge so the seam is exactly on the lower edge of the rod. A wide heading may be made to look puffy and more rounded by pulling the fabric out on each side.

31

How to Sew a Continental™ or Cornice Rod Casing with a Heading

1) Measure window after rod has been installed to determine total length. Add 15½" (39.3 cm): 5½" (14 cm) for the casing and seam allowance, 8" (20.5 cm) for the double-fold hem, and 2" (5 cm) for 1" (2.5 cm) heading. For a deeper heading, add twice the desired heading depth.

2) Turn under ½" (1.3 cm) on upper edge of curtain and press. Fold over again 6" (15 cm) for casing and heading. Stitch 1" (2.5 cm) from upper folded edge to form heading. Stitch close to folded edge to form casing.

3) Insert rod through casing and gather curtain evenly onto rod. Hang on installed brackets. For a wide heading, use two Continental or cornice rods, installed one above the other. Add 10" (25.5 cm) for second casing.

How to Make a Shirred Pole Cover

1) Cut fabric two and one-half times the length of pole area to be covered; cut width equal to circumference of pole plus 1½" (3.8 cm). For pole cover with a heading, add amount equal to twice the heading depth.

2) Stitch ½" (1.3 cm) hems on short ends. Fold strip in half lengthwise, right sides together, and pin long edges together. Stitch ½" (1.3 cm) seam. Press seam open. Turn cover right side out.

3) Press cover so that seam is at back of pole. To form heading, stitch again at appropriate distance from upper folded edge. If desired, add narrow binding to upper edge, opposite. Gather pole cover onto rod between two curtain panels.

Customizing Casing-top Curtains

Bindings, borders, ribbon or contrasting returns give casings individuality and style. These decorative touches customize casings and require little additional sewing time.

Contrasting returns. Cut fabric strips the width of return plus 1" (2.5 cm), and the cut length of curtain. Allow for ½" (1.3 cm) side seam on one edge of the curtain. Press under ½" (1.3 cm) on one long edge of strip. Pin right side of strip to wrong side of curtain, unpressed raw edges even; stitch. Press strip to right side; fuse or edgestitch edge to right side of curtain. Finish curtain.

Narrow binding. Construct basic curtain. Cut 2½" (6.5 cm) strip of fabric with length equal to finished width of panel plus 1" (2.5 cm). Press under ½" (1.3 cm) on one long side and each short end. Pin unpressed edge to upper edge of curtain, right sides together; stitch. Press folded edge of binding over upper edge. From right side, stitch in the ditch.

Edgestitched ribbon banding. Cut fabric trims two times the finished width of banding, length equal to cut length of curtain. Press and stitch 1" (2.5 cm) double-fold side hems on curtain. Press trim, wrong sides together and raw edges meeting at center. Pin trim with outer edge covering side hem stitching line. Edgestitch trim close to folded edges. Finish curtain.

Fused border. Construct basic curtain. Cut fabric trim two times the width of finished band, and the finished length of curtain plus 1" (2.5 cm). Press trim wrong sides together and raw edges meeting at center; press under ½" (1.3 cm) on short ends. Cut strips of fusible web slightly narrower than finished trim; insert between curtain and trim. Fuse in place.

Lining Curtains

Linings add body and weight to curtains to help them hang better. A lining also adds opaqueness, prevents fading and sun damage to curtain fabric, and provides some insulation.

Curtains may be lined the traditional way or lined to the edge with coordinating fabric to create a custom look.

Select linings according to the weight of the curtain fabric. White or off-white sateen is the most often used lining fabric. Specially treated linings that resist staining and block out light are also available.

✂ Cutting Directions

For a lined curtain with a casing, cut the curtain as directed on page 27. For lining with 2" (5 cm) double-fold hem, cut lining the finished length of curtain plus 2½" (6.5 cm); cut lining 6" (15 cm) narrower than cut width of curtain. Seam and press widths, aligning curtain and lining seams if possible.

For curtains lined to the edge, cut curtain and lining the finished length plus amount for double-fold hem and ½" (1.3 cm) for seam at upper edge. Cut panels the finished width plus 1" (2.5 cm) for side seams.

How to Line Curtains

1) **Turn,** press and stitch 2" (5 cm) double-fold hem in lining. Turn and press double-fold hem in curtain. Tack weights inside fold of curtain hems at seams and stitch curtain hems.

2) **Place** lining on curtain, right sides together, so lining is 1½" (3.8 cm) above curtain hem. Pin and stitch ½" (1.3 cm) seams on sides.

3) **Turn** curtain right side out. Center lining so side hems are equal width. Press side hem with seam allowance toward center. Continue to the top edge of the curtain.

4) **Press** ½" (1.3 cm) seam allowance across upper edge of curtain. Fold upper edge of curtain down an amount equal to depth of casing and heading. Lining ends at foldline.

5) Stitch close to the folded edge to form casing. For curtains with headings, stitch the heading the desired depth.

6) Hand-tack weights along lower edge of curtain inside side hems.

7) Turn side hems back diagonally below lining to form a miter. Slipstitch miter in place.

8) Make French tacks about 12" (30.5 cm) apart between hem and lining, using double thread. Take two stitches near top of hem and directly across in lining, leaving 1" (2.5 cm) slack in thread. Make blanket stitch over thread; secure with knot in lining.

How to Line Curtains to the Edge

1) Cut curtain and lining the same size. Turn, press and stitch equal lower hems in curtain and lining. Place right sides of curtain and lining together with lower hems even. Pin sides and upper edge.

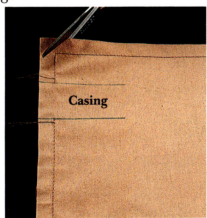

Casing

2) Mark casing and heading depth on lining. Join lining and curtain with ½" (1.3 cm) seam on sides and upper edge, leaving opening on both sides at casing line. Diagonally trim upper corners. Press the upper seam open.

3) Turn curtain right side out. Press seams flat. Stitch casing and heading. Insert curtain rod in casing. Hang curtain and fold lining to right side so contrasting fabric shows; secure with tieback.

Tab Top Curtains

Fabric tabs are an attractive alternative to conventional casings or curtain rings. Tab top curtains used with a decorative curtain rod create a traditional country look, a contemporary tailored look or a casual cafe look. They are also ideal for stationary side panels. Tabs give top interest to a curtain, and can be made with contrasting fabric, decorative ribbon or trim.

Only one and one-half to two times the fullness is needed for tab top curtains. Allow ½" (1.3 cm) seam allowance at the upper edge of the curtain instead of the usual casing allowance. When determining the finished length, allow for the upper edge of the curtain to be 1½" to 2" (3.8 to 5 cm) below the rod. This determines the length of the tabs. Determine number of tabs needed by placing a tab at each edge of the curtain, and space the remaining tabs 6" to 8" (15 to 20.5 cm) apart.

How to Sew Tab Top Curtains

1) Cut a 3" (7.5 cm) facing strip equal in length to the width of the curtain panel. Press under ½" (1.3 cm) on one long side and each short end. Press double-fold lower and side hems of curtain. Stitch lower hem only.

2) Measure tab length by pinning a strip of fabric over the rod and marking the desired length with a pin. Add ½" (1.3 cm) for seam allowance. Cut tabs to measured length, and two times the desired width plus 1" (2.5 cm).

3) Fold each tab in half lengthwise, right sides together. Stitch ½" (1.3 cm) seam along cut edge; sew from one tab to the next, using continuous stitching (arrow). Turn tabs right side out. Center seam in back of each tab; press.

4) Fold each tab in half so raw edges are aligned. Pin or baste tabs in place on right side of curtain, aligning raw edges of tabs with upper edge of curtain. Place end tabs even with side hem foldline of curtain.

5) Pin facing to upper edge of curtain, right sides together, so raw edges are aligned and tabs are sandwiched between facing and curtain. Stitch ½" (1.3 cm) seam, with curtain side hems extended.

6) Press facing to wrong side of curtain so tabs extend upward. Fold curtain side hems under facing, covering seam allowance; grade. Stitch side hems. Slipstitch facing to curtain. Insert curtain rod through tabs.

Ruffled Curtains

Ruffled curtains add a charming, warm touch to any room of the house, and the weight of ruffles helps curtains hang better. The ruffle on a curtain usually extends along one side and across the bottom. In the directions that follow the curtain is hemmed after the ruffle is attached, and the ruffle extends into the casing and heading. A coordinated shirred valance (page 65) may be added for a decorative touch.

Ruffle fullness depends on fabric weight and ruffle width. Sheer fabrics usually need triple fullness; crisper fabrics need only two or two and one-half times fullness. Wide ruffles should be fuller than narrow ruffles. You will usually need to purchase less additional fabric when ruffles are cut on the crosswise grain. If ruffles are cut on the selvage, use the selvage edge in the seam. Hem the edge of the ruffle before gathering.

Single ruffles are one layer of gathered fabric with a hemmed edge. Narrow ruffles should have a hem no wider than ¼" (6 mm).

Double ruffles require a double width of fabric which is folded in half, wrong sides together. The folded edge eliminates the need for a hem. Because of the extra bulk created by two layers, it is best to make double ruffles from lightweight fabrics.

The zigzag stitch, the ruffler and the narrow hemmer can speed up the task of making ruffles. Begin by cutting the fabric the appropriate width for a single or double ruffle. Then seam sections together at the short ends to make a continuous length, using plain seams for double ruffles and French seams for single ruffles. Hem one long edge of single ruffles, either by machine-stitching a double-fold ¼" (6 mm) hem, or by using a narrow hemmer.

Two Timesaving Ways to Make Ruffles

Zigzag over a strong, thin cord on wrong side of fabric to make long ruffles easier to adjust into even gathers. Use cord, crochet cotton or dental floss, placed ⅜" (1 cm) from raw edge. Use wide zigzag stitch so cord does not get caught in the stitching.

Use a ruffler attachment to tuck or gather as you sew. Make a test strip and adjust ruffler to desired fullness. Measure the test strip before and after stitching to determine length of fabric needed. Omit steps 1 through 3 (opposite) when using ruffler.

How to Attach Ruffles

1) **Divide** curtain edge into equal segments; mark with pins. Divide ruffle strip into same number of segments. Allow extra fullness in segments to be placed at corner, so ruffle will lie flat in finished curtain.

2) **Pin** the ruffle strip to the unhemmed edge of the curtain, right sides together; match marking pins on the ruffle strip to marking pins on the curtain edge.

3) **Pull** up gathering cord until ruffle is same size as edge of curtain. At lower edge, release gathers the depth of hem. At upper edge, release gathers the depth of casing and heading.

4) **Pin** in place as necessary to distribute gathers evenly. Stitch a ½" (1.3 cm) seam, gathered side up, controlling gathers with fingers on each side of the needle.

5) **Trim** seam allowances and overedge (**a**) using zigzag stitch, or encase seam with double-fold bias tape (**b**), or encase seam with lightweight bias tricot strips (**c**).

6) **Press** seam toward curtain. Topstitch on curtain side ¼" (6 mm) from seam so ruffle will lie smooth and even. Stitch hem and casing. Ruffle is gathered on right side, but flat on wrong side.

Tiebacks

Tiebacks are a decorative way to hold curtains open. Make them straight or shaped, ruffled or plain. Use matching or contrasting solids, coordinating prints or bordered fabrics. Interface all tiebacks to add stability.

An easy way to make tiebacks the proper length is to complete and hang the curtains before sewing the tiebacks. Cut a strip of fabric that is 2" to 4" (5 to 10 cm) wide; experiment by pinning it around the curtains to determine the best tieback length. Slide the strip up and down to find the best location for tiebacks. Mark the wall for positioning cup hooks, which will be used to fasten the tiebacks. Remove the strip and measure it to determine the finished size.

✂ Cutting Directions

For straight tiebacks, cut a piece of heavyweight fusible interfacing the finished length and two times the finished width. To cut fabric, add ½" (1.3 cm) on all sides for seams.

For shaped tiebacks, cut a strip of brown paper for pattern, 4" to 6" (10 to 15 cm) wide and slightly longer than the tieback. Pin the paper around the curtain and draw a curved shape around the edge of the paper. Experiment by pinning and trimming the paper to get the effect you want. Cut two pieces of fabric and heavyweight fusible interfacing for each tieback. Cut interfacing same size as pattern. To cut fabric, add ½" (1.3 cm) on all sides for seams.

YOU WILL NEED

Decorator fabric for tiebacks.

Heavyweight fusible interfacing.

Brown paper for pattern.

Fusible web strips, length of finished tieback width.

Two ⅝" (1.5 cm) brass or plastic rings for each tieback.

Two cup hooks.

How to Sew Straight Tiebacks

1) Center fusible interfacing on wrong side of tieback and fuse. Press the short ends under ½" (1.3 cm). Fold tieback in half lengthwise, right sides together. Stitch ½" (1.3 cm) seam, leaving short ends open. Press open.

2) Turn tieback right side out. Center seam down back and press. Turn pressed ends inside. Insert fusible web at each end and fuse. Or slipstitch closed.

3) Hand-tack ring on back seamline at each end of tieback, ¼" (6 mm) from edge **(a)**. Or press corners diagonally to inside to form a point; slipstitch or fuse corners in place. Attach ring **(b)**.

How to Sew Shaped Tiebacks

1) Position pattern on fold to cut fabric and interfacing. Center interfacing on wrong side of each tieback piece and fuse.

2) Pin tieback pieces, right sides together. Stitch ½" (1.3 cm) seam, leaving 4" (10 cm) opening on one long edge for turning. Grade seam allowances; notch or clip curves at regular intervals.

3) Turn tieback right side out; press. Insert fusible web at opening and fuse. Or slipstitch closed. Hand-tack rings at each end of tieback ¼" (6 mm) from the edge.

Bound Tiebacks

Binding emphasizes the graceful line of a curved tieback and allows you to pick up an accent color from the room decor or from the curtain fabric. Shaped tiebacks are easier to bind than straight tiebacks because the bias binding will ease around curves.

✄ Cutting Directions

Cut two pieces of fabric and two pieces of fusible interfacing from the pattern; do not add seam allowances to tieback. Make bias tape as on page 74. Cut the tape 1" (2.5 cm) longer than the distance around the tieback.

How to Bind Shaped Tiebacks

1) Position pattern on fold to cut fabric and interfacing. Fuse interfacing to wrong side of tieback. Pin wrong sides of tieback together.

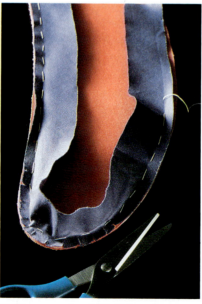

2) Press under ½" (1.3 cm) on one end of bias strip. Starting with pressed end, baste strip to tieback, right sides together, clipping to ease around curves. Stitch strip ½" (1.3 cm) from edge.

3) Press bias strip over edge of tieback. Turn under cut edge of bias strip to meet seamline; slipstitch. Hand-tack rings to ends of tieback.

Ruffled Tiebacks

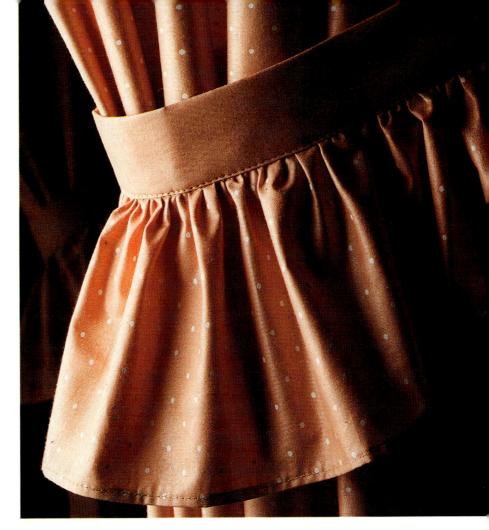

Adding ruffled tiebacks changes the appearance of the curtains and the look of a window. Make ruffles from a matching or coordinating fabric in a width that suits the length of the curtain. Purchased pregathered lace or eyelet ruffles may be used to reduce sewing time.

✂ Cutting Directions

Cut ruffle the desired width plus 1" (2.5 cm) for seams, and two and one-half times the finished length.

Cut a straight tieback and interfacing (page 40). The tieback should be in proportion to the ruffle width, usually less than half as wide.

How to Sew Ruffled Tiebacks

1) Fuse interfacing to wrong side of tieback. Press under ½" (1.3 cm) on one long side and both ends of tieback. Stitch a ¼" (6 mm) hem on one long side and both ends of ruffle. Fold ruffle and tieback into fourths; mark folds with snips.

2) Zigzag over a cord (page 38). Pin wrong side of ruffle to right side of tieback, matching snips and raw edges. Pull up gathering cord until ruffle fits tieback. Distribute gathers evenly and pin. Stitch ruffle ½" (1.3 cm) from edge.

3) Fold tieback in half lengthwise, wrong sides together. Pin the folded edge over ruffle seam. Edgestitch across ends and along gathered seam. Hand-tack the rings to ends of tieback.

Shower Curtain

A shower curtain is one of the simplest curtains to sew. Valances and tiebacks can be used with the standard shower curtain. Because of its size, the shower curtain is a good place to use bold colors and prints. The instructions for sewing a shower curtain can also be used for cafe curtains or straight curtains hung with rings or hooks on decorative poles.

✄ Cutting Directions

Measure the distance from the bottom of the shower rod to the desired length. Add 10" (25.5 cm) for upper and lower hems. Measure the width of the area to be covered by the curtain and add 4" (10 cm) for side hems. Standard shower curtain liners are 72" × 72" (183 × 183 cm), so the curtain should be cut 76" (193 cm) wide if using a standard liner. Seam fabric together as needed, using French seams.

YOU WILL NEED

Decorator fabric for shower curtain.

Fusible interfacing.

Plastic shower curtain liner.

Eyelets or grommets (not necessary if buttonholes are used), equal to number of holes in plastic liner.

Shower curtain hooks, equal to number of eyelets or buttonholes.

The fabric curtain and plastic liner can hang together on the same rings or hooks, or separately on a shower rod and a spring tension rod. When they hang together, the shower curtain and the liner should be the same width.

How to Sew a Shower Curtain

1) Turn under and stitch a 3" (7.5 cm) double-fold hem on lower edge of curtain. Turn under and stitch 1" (2.5 cm) double-fold hem on each side of the curtain.

2) Press under 2" (5 cm) double-fold hem at upper edge of curtain. Open out fold and fuse a 2" (5 cm) strip of fusible interfacing along foldline. Fold again to form a double-fold hem.

3) Edgestitch upper hem in place. Or apply fusible web, following the manufacturer's directions. Fusing adds more stability to upper edge of curtain.

4) Mark positions for eyelets, grommets or buttonholes across upper hem, using the plastic liner as the guide for spacing holes. Position liner ¼" (6 mm) down from upper edge of curtain.

5a) Fasten eyelets securely using eyelet set and hammer or eyelet pliers. If using eyelet set, work on a piece of scrap wood or a hard surface that will not be damaged when pounding eyelets.

5b) Make vertical buttonholes, ¼" to ½" (6 mm to 1.3 cm) long. To prevent buttonholes from raveling, apply liquid fray preventer to cut edges. Insert rings or hooks.

Shades

Shades control light and provide privacy when used alone or with curtains. Because they fit close to windows, shades are also energy efficient.

Shades can be mounted either inside or outside the window frame. The screws can be inserted on either the 1" or 2" (2.5 or 5 cm) side of the mounting board. This will determine how far from the window your shade will hang.

Roman shade is the basis for stitched-tuck, hobbled, cloud, balloon and insulated shades. These shades are raised and lowered by a system of cords and rings which cause them to pleat into soft folds when raised.

Stitched-tuck shade has small, topstitched tucks along the folds of the shade. These tucked rows alternate between the front and the back of the shade, giving the pleats a crisp look.

Hobbled shade is two times the length of a flat Roman shade. Excess fabric is taken up in permanent soft folds between each row of rings, giving the shade a bubbled look when lowered.

Cloud shade is cut two to three times the width of the window, then shirred across the upper edge to create a soft heading. The lower edge of the shade falls into gentle poufs.

Balloon shade is also cut two to two and one-half times the width of the window, but its fullness is folded into oversized inverted pleats at the heading and lower edge. This shade also has permanent poufs at the bottom.

Insulated shade is a basic Roman shade made with insulated lining and a magnetic edge-seal. These shades block out heat or cold, and help regulate temperature extremes at windows.

Roller shade takes on a custom look when made to coordinate with fabrics in the room. These shades, stiffened with a fusible shade backing, are easy to make because they require very little sewing.

Two Ways to Mount Shades

Angle irons

Screws

Inside mounted shade fits completely inside window opening. Accurate construction and mounting is important. Attach shade to 1" × 2" (2.5 × 5 cm) mounting board; then attach board to top of window frame with angle irons or screws. Finished width and length of shade are equal to width and length of window opening.

Outside mounted shade is attached to mounting board, which is secured with screws or angle irons above the window. Finished shade is the same width as the mounting board and covers the frame when lowered. Finished shade length equals distance from top of board to sill or apron. Use this method for windows of different sizes or out-of-square windows.

Roman Shade

Roman shades have a tailored appearance that complements many styles of decor. Use them alone or add cornices, curtains or draperies.

Like roller shades, Roman shades are flat and smooth when down. When pulled up, they take up more space at the top because they pleat crisply instead of rolling. If you want the raised shade to clear the window completely, mount it at the ceiling. This also adds apparent height to the window. A system of evenly-spaced cords and rings on the back of the shade causes the shade to pleat when pulled. A weight bar near the bottom of the shade adds stability and aids smooth tracking.

The choice of fabric affects the look of the finished shade. Sturdy, firm fabrics work best for the pleats of these shades. Lightweight, softer fabrics may be used, but the shades will be less crisp-looking. Roman shades are usually lined. This gives added body to the shade, prevents fabric fading and gives windows a uniform appearance from the outside.

You may need to seam fabric or lining to create enough width for the shades. Be sure to consider these seams when measuring for construction. Additional fabric may be needed to match a print, plaid or other design.

To make measuring and construction easier and more accurate, use a folding cardboard cutting board on your work surface.

✂ Cutting Directions

Determine width and length of finished shade. Cut decorator fabric for shade 3" (7.5 cm) wider and 3" (7.5 cm) longer than finished shade.

Cut lining with width equal to finished width of shade; length equal to finished length plus 3" (7.5 cm).

Cut facing strip from lining fabric, 5" (12.5 cm) wide; length equal to finished width of shade plus 2" (5 cm).

YOU WILL NEED

Decorator fabric for shade.

Lining fabric for lining and facing strip.

Mounting board, 1" × 2" (2.5 × 5 cm), cut to size for inside or outside mounting (page 47). Paint ends of board or cover with matching fabric.

Screw eyes or pulleys, large enough to hold all the pull cords. Number should equal the number of vertical rows.

Shade cord for each vertical row of rings. Each cord must be long enough to go up the shade, across the top and partway down the side for pulling.

Plastic rings, ½" (1.3 cm), equal to number of vertical rows multiplied by number of horizontal rows. Or use ring tape with 6" (15 cm) spaces the length of the shade times the number of vertical rows plus 6" (15 cm) for each row.

Weight rod, one ⅜" (1 cm) brass rod or ½" (1.3 cm) rustproof flat bar, cut ½" (1.3 cm) shorter than finished width of shade.

White glue or liquid fray preventer.

Awning cleat.

Staple gun or tacks.

Drapery pull (optional).

How to Make a Roman Shade

1) Sketch the shade to use as a guide for ring locations, page 50, step 7. Cut shade fabric; seam for width, if necessary. If fabric ravels, finish side edges with zigzag stitch or liquid fray preventer.

2) Place shade fabric wrong side up on work surface. Mark finished width. Press 1½" (3.8 cm) side hems.

3) Place lining on shade fabric, wrong sides together. Slip lining under side hems. Smooth and press lining. Pin in place; slipstitch, if desired.

4) Center and pin facing strip on right side of shade, even with lower edge, with 1" (2.5 cm) extending at each side. Stitch ½" (1.3 cm) from lower edge. Press toward wrong side of shade.

5) Fold and press facing extensions to back of shade so they do not show on the right side. Fuse or stitch in place.

6) Turn under raw edge of facing 1½" (3.8 cm); turn under again 3" (7.5 cm). Stitch along folded edge. Stitch again, 1" (2.5 cm) from first stitching to form pocket for weight rod.

(Continued on next page.)

7) Mark locations for rings with horizontal and vertical rows of X's. First, mark outside vertical rows 1" (2.5 cm) from shade edges so rings hold side hems in place. Space vertical rows 8" to 12" (20.5 to 30.5 cm) apart across shade. Position bottom row just above the rod pocket. Space horizontal rows 5" to 8" (12.5 to 20.5 cm) apart.

8) Pin through both layers of fabric at center of ring markings, with pins parallel to bottom of shade. Fold shade in accordion pleats at pins to position shade for machine or hand stitching of rings. If using ring tape, omit steps 9a and 9b.

9c) Use ring tape instead of rings, if desired. Turn under ½" (1.3 cm) at bottom of tape and place at top of rod pocket. Pin tape to shade in vertical rows, lining up rings horizontally. Stitch both long edges and bottom of tape with zipper foot, stitching all tapes in same direction.

10) Staple or tack shade to top of mounting board. If shade is mounted outside of window frame, paint or wrap the board with lining fabric before attaching shade. This gives the shade a finished look.

13) Cut lengths of cord, one for each row of rings. Each cord will be a different length; cords go up the shade, across the top and partway down one side. String cord through rings and screw eyes, with excess cord at one side for pulling.

14) File ends of weight rod or cover ends with tape. Insert rod into rod pocket and slipstitch ends closed. A galvanized or iron rod, painted to resist rusting, can be used instead of a brass rod.

9a) Attach rings by placing fold (pin in center) under presser foot with ring next to fold. Set stitch length at 0, and zigzag at widest setting. Secure ring with 8 to 10 stitches, catching small amount of fold in each stitch. Lock stitches by adjusting needle to penetrate fabric in one place (width setting at 0) for 2 or 3 stitches.

9b) Tack rings by hand if zigzag stitch is not available. Use double thread. Secure with 4 or 5 stitches in one place, through both fabric layers. Reinforce all rings in bottom row with extra stitches; they hold the weight of the fabric.

11) Insert screw eyes on mounting board to line up with vertical rows; place one screw eye above each row. On heavy or wide shades, use pulleys instead of screw eyes.

12) Tie a nonslip knot in bottom ring. Apply white glue to knot and ends of cord to prevent knot from slipping. Thread cord through the vertical row of rings.

15) Mount shade (page 47). Adjust cords with shade lowered so the tension on each cord is equal. Tie cords in a knot just below screw eye. Braid cords and secure at bottom with a knot or drapery pull.

16) Center awning cleat on edge of window frame or on wall. Wind cord around cleat to secure shade position when the shade is raised.

Stitched-tuck Shade

Narrow stitched tucks along each fold line add interest to this tailored version of the Roman shade. Read about Roman shades on pages 48 to 51 before beginning this project.

To determine the number of tucks, subtract 3" (7.5 cm) for the hem from finished length of shade. Divide this number by 3" (7.5 cm), the approximate spacing between tucks, to get the number of tucks. Round this figure to the nearest whole number. To determine the spacing between tucks, divide the finished length of shade by the number of tucks (as determined above). Rings will be placed on alternate tucks, beginning with the bottom tuck.

✂ Cutting Directions

Cut decorator fabric and lining as for Roman shade (page 48), adding ½" (1.3 cm) for each tuck to the length of both fabrics. Also cut facing strip from lining fabric, 5" (12.5 cm) wide; length equal to finished shade width plus 2" (5 cm).

YOU WILL NEED

Decorator fabric for shade.

Lining fabric for lining and facing strip.

Notions: mounting board, plastic rings, screws eyes or pulleys, shade cord, weight rod, white glue, awning cleat and staple gun, as for Roman shade.

How to Make a Stitched-tuck Shade

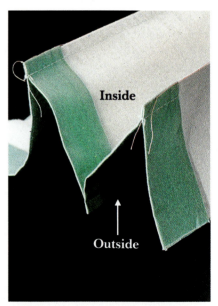

1) Follow directions for Roman shade, pages 49 and 50, steps 1 to 7, except space horizontal rows as figured above. Draw horizontal lines across wrong side of shade at ring locations. Baste lining and outer fabric together on each line.

2) Remove water-soluble pen markings. Fold and press sharp crease exactly on each basting line, right sides together. Bring opposite folds together, accordion pleat style, and press crease in each fold. Machine-baste as in step 1.

3) Stitch tucks ¼" (6 mm) from creased edges on right side and wrong side of shade. Complete the shade following the directions for a Roman shade, pages 50 and 51, steps 9a to 16. Do not use ring tape.

Hobbled Shade

The hobbled shade falls into soft folds because it is twice the length of the Roman shade. The folds are held in place by twill tape. Read about Roman shades (pages 48 to 51) before beginning this project.

To determine the number of folds, subtract 3" (7.5 cm) for the hem from finished length of shade. Divide this number by 6" (15 cm), the approximate spacing between folds, to get the number of folds. Round this figure to the nearest whole number. To determine the spacing between folds, divide the finished length of the shade by the number of folds (as determined above).

✄ Cutting Directions

Cut decorator fabric and lining as for Roman shade (page 48), doubling the length for both fabrics. Cut facing strip from lining fabric, 5" (12.5 cm) wide; length equal to finished shade width plus 2" (5 cm). Cut twill tape, length equal to finished shade length plus 3" (7.5 cm).

YOU WILL NEED

Decorator fabric for shade.

Lining fabric for lining and facing strip.

Twill tape ½" (1.3 cm) wide.

Notions: mounting board, plastic rings, screw eyes or pulleys, shade cord, weight rod, white glue, awning cleat and staple gun, as for Roman shade.

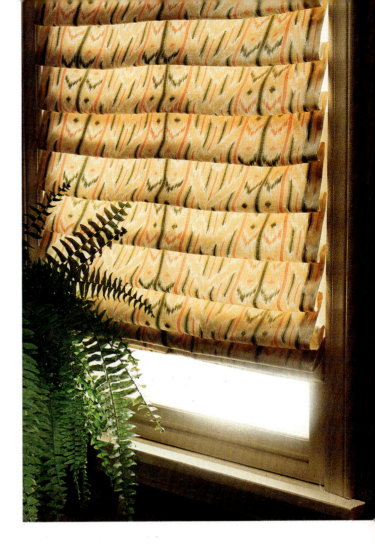

How to Make a Hobbled Shade

1) Follow directions for Roman shade, pages 49 and 50, steps 1 to 7, except space horizontal rows as figured above. Align tapes with shade; mark tapes at intervals halfway between rings on shade, beginning at top of rod pocket.

2) Pin tapes to the shade, lining up marks on tapes with marks on shade. The excess fabric between the markings forms folds on the right side of the shade.

3) Tack the rings in place, catching the tape and both layers of the fabric at each ring. Complete shade following directions for Roman shade, pages 50 and 51, steps 10 to 16.

Cloud Shade

The cloud shade is another easy-to-make variation of the Roman shade with a soft shirred heading. Because this shade has a light, airy look, lining is usually not necessary. Lightweight, soft or sheer fabrics are suggested for cloud shades.

Cloud shades are generally mounted inside the window and may be used alone or under draperies. The shade's shirred heading has a finished look that makes a valance or cornice unnecessary. A short cloud shade may also be used as a valance over other window treatments.

Cloud shades made of lightweight fabrics may be shirred on a curtain rod or wooden pole, omitting the need for a mounting board. In this case, finish the upper edge of the shade with a simple casing (page 31) and insert screw eyes directly into the window frame.

Directions for making a cloud shade are given on pages 56 and 57. Read about Roman shades on pages 48 to 51 before beginning this project.

✂ Cutting Directions
Cut decorator fabric so width of shade is two to three times width of window and about 12" (30.5 cm) longer than window. Seam fabric together as necessary for desired width. Also cut facing strip 4" (10 cm) wide; the length equal to the width of the finished shade plus 1" (2.5 cm).

YOU WILL NEED

Decorator fabric for shade and facing strip.

Four-cord shirring tape, length equal to width of shade.

Notions: mounting board, plastic rings, screw eyes or pulleys, shade cord, weight rod, white glue, awning cleat and staple gun, as for Roman shade.

Balloon Shade

The balloon shade is another variation of the Roman shade. A series of evenly placed box pleats gives this shade a fuller, softer effect than the more tailored Roman shade.

Made from soft, sheer or unlined fabrics, balloon shades drape into gentle poufs or swags. With sturdier fabrics, the softness remains but the fabric may require hand dressing to even out the fullness.

Linings are optional. Follow the directions for a lined Roman shade, page 49, step 3, if opaqueness or additional body is required.

Directions for making a balloon shade are given on pages 56 and 57. Read about Roman shades on pages 48 to 51 before beginning this project.

✂ Cutting Directions

Cut decorator fabric so width of shade is two to two and one-half times width of window and about 12" (30.5 cm) longer than window. Seam together as necessary for desired width, positioning the seam at the inside fold of a pleat. Also cut facing strip 3" (7.5 cm) wide and the length equal to the width of finished shade plus 1" (2.5 cm).

Make a paper pattern to help you position the pleats accurately on the shade. Make pattern by cutting a narrow strip of paper, such as adding machine paper, the same length as the unfinished width of the shade.

YOU WILL NEED

Decorator fabric for shade and facing strip.

Lining fabric for lining (optional).

Notions: mounting board, plastic rings, screw eyes or pulleys, shade cord, weight rod, white glue, awning cleat and staple gun, as for Roman shade.

How to Make a Cloud Shade

1) Seam fabric if necessary for width, using French seams. Turn under and press 1" (2.5 cm) double-fold side and lower hems. Straight-stitch or blindstitch hems.

2) Turn under 3¾" (9.5 cm) at upper edge. Pin shirring tape ¼" (6 mm) from fold. Pull out ½" (1.3 cm) of cord at each end; turn tape under to finish ends. Using zipper foot, stitch on each side of cord. (Contrasting thread is used to show detail.)

5) Pull other ends of cords until shade gathers up to width of mounting board. Knot, glue and trim pulled cord ends as in step 4, above.

6) Press under ½" (1.3 cm) on short ends of facing strip. Fold strip in half lengthwise, wrong sides together. Pin raw edges of strip to right side of shade above shirring tape; stitch ½" (1.3 cm) from edge. Staple strip to top of mounting board.

How to Make a Balloon Shade

1) Prepare fabric as in step 1, above, but do not hem lower edge. Fold pleats in pattern 9" to 12" (23 to 30.5 cm) apart and about 6" (15 cm) deep. Use even number of pleats with half pleat at each side.

2) Place paper pattern on shade at lower edge. Place seams at back folds of pleats. Mark pleat fold lines with ¼" (6 mm) snips. Repeat this step along the upper edge of the shade.

3) Fold, pin and press pleats the entire length of shade. Stitch ½" (1.3 cm) from upper and lower edges to secure pleats. Stitch again 3" (7.5 cm) from upper edge for mounting guideline.

3) **Mark** positions for rings. Space horizontal rows about 6" (15 cm) apart. Space vertical rows 18" to 36" (46 to 91.5 cm) apart; rows will be half that distance apart when shirring tape is gathered. Attach rings, page 51, step 9a or 9b.

4) **Knot** ends of shirring cords along one edge of shade to keep the cords from pulling out. Apply white glue to knots so they stay in place. Trim ends.

7) **Tie** together bottom three rings of each vertical row. This creates a permanent pouf in the shade, even when it is completely lowered. String and mount as for Roman shades, pages 50 and 51, steps 13, 15 and 16.

8) **Cover** the weight rod with matching fabric. Insert rod in lower hem. Gather fabric evenly on the rod to correspond to gathers on upper edge. Slipstitch ends of hem closed.

4) **Press** under ½" (1.3 cm) on short ends of facing strip; press in half lengthwise, wrong sides together. Pin strip to bottom of shade on right side. Stitch ½" (1.3 cm) from edge for rod pocket; finish seam.

5) **Press** strip to wrong side. Attach rings through one layer at center of pleats, with bottom rings on facing fold and top rings below guideline, page 51, step 9a or 9b. Vertical rows should be about 6" (15 cm) apart.

6) **Staple** upper edge of shade to mounting board, with mounting guideline at the upper edge of mounting board so stitching does not show. Finish as for cloud shade, steps 7 and 8, above.

Roller Shade

Mount roller shades inside the window opening with ¼" (6 mm) or less clearance around the edges to increase the energy efficiency of a window. Roller shades can also be hung on brackets on the frame or wall outside the window. For inside mounting, measure from outside edges of brackets. If you do not want the roller to show, use reverse brackets, and cut the roller to fit.

Select a firmly woven fabric that bonds well. Water-resistant and stain-resistant fabrics that are treated with silicone do not bond.

✂ **Cutting Directions**

Cut fabric 1" to 2" (2.5 to 5 cm) wider than jamb or bracket measurement, and 12" (30.5 cm) longer than area to be covered top to bottom. Cut fusible backing with same dimensions.

YOU WILL NEED

Fabric and fusible shade backing for shade.

Wooden slat, ¼" (6 mm) shorter than finished width of shade.

Roller to fit window width.

Staple gun with ¼" (6 mm) staples, masking tape or other strong tape and white glue.

Shade pull (optional).

How to Make a Roller Shade

1) Mark center at upper and lower edges of fabric and fusible backing. Place the wrong side of the fabric to the resin side of the backing, matching edges and center markings.

2) Fuse according to manufacturer's directions for time and temperature, working from center to outside and from top to bottom. Allow shade to cool before moving so bond is permanently set.

3) Use a yardstick to mark cutting lines on sides of shade; distance between cutting lines should be equal to finished width of shade. Use a carpenter's square or cutting board for right angles.

4) Cut carefully along cutting lines with smooth, even strokes. To keep edges from raveling, put a small amount of white glue on your finger and draw it along each edge. Let dry completely.

5) Fold under 1½" (3.8 cm) along lower edge for a straight hem and slat pocket. Use carpenter's square to check right angles at corners.

6) Stitch 1¼" (3.2 cm) from folded edge, using long stitches to form a pocket for the slat. Press pocket. Insert the slat. Attach shade pull if desired.

7) Position roller under or over top of shade, depending on how shade is to roll. To attach roller under shade, place flat pin to the right **(a)**; to attach roller over shade, place round pin to the right **(b)**. Make sure wrong side of hem is turned so it will not show when shade is hung. Staple or tape shade to roller.

Insulated Roman Shade

Insulated Roman shades are practical for sewers who are energy conscious. These shades help your home stay warm in winter and cool in summer; they pay for themselves in reduced heating and cooling costs. Read about Roman shades on pages 48 to 51 before beginning this project.

The shades are lined with insulated lining, the portion of the shade that provides effective insulation when the shade is lowered. Insulated lining consists of four layers (see below), quilted in 8" (20.5 cm) channels, with 4" (10 cm) channels at the edges.

Because the insulating layers are quilted, the time-consuming task of making your own layers is eliminated. Quilting also reduces bulk, making the finished shade more attractive and easier to handle.

The quilting lines mark the horizontal ring positions on the Roman shade. (Channels run on the *lengthwise* grain of the fabric but *crosswise* on the finished shade.) This eliminates much of the measuring normally required to mark ring positions.

Combined with an edge-seal system, insulated shades can reduce heat loss and heat gain from windows even more effectively. An edge-seal system consists of flexible magnetic strips placed along the sides of the window and inside the shade edges. On closed shades, these strips form an airtight seal which keeps warm, moist air from flowing around the edges of the shade, causing energy loss and condensation. The magnetic strips may be painted to match the window frame.

Before making the shade, decide how it will be mounted to determine the length and width of the finished shade. The three types of mounts that may be used for insulated Roman shades are *inside, outside* and *hybrid*. Descriptions of inside and outside mounts are given on pages 47 and 64.

The hybrid mount (page 64) is especially good for insulated shades. Although the mounting board is cut and mounted like an inside mount, the shade is about ¾" (2 cm) wider on each side and overlaps the window to control airflow around the edges.

✂ Cutting Directions

Cut fabric for shade 3" (7.5 cm) wider and 12" (30.5 cm) longer than finished shade. Cut insulated lining with width equal to finished width of shade; length equal to finished length plus about 4" (10 cm) for mounting.

YOU WILL NEED

Decorator fabric for shade.

Insulated lining, channel quilted.

Magnetic tape for edge-seal system.

Notions: Mounting board, plastic rings, screw eyes, pulley or pulley lock, shade cord, weight rod, awning cleat, glue and staple gun, as for Roman shade.

Insulated lining consists of four layers: cotton/polyester lining (**a**); polyester batting (**b**); polyethelene moisture vapor barrier (**c**); heat-reflecting Mylar® (**d**). With the addition of the decorator fabric (**e**), the shade provides five layers of insulation.

Splice for added length by joining two pieces on quilting lines. This maintains 8" (20.5 cm) between lines. Stitch through all layers, applying slight tension in front of and behind needle. Trim and grade seam to ¼" (6 mm), holding scissors at an angle.

Edge-seal system consists of strips of magnetic tape placed on the window frame to correspond to strips of tape placed inside the shade. When pressed together, magnetic strips form a seal that shuts out hot or cold air. To release seal, pull shade out at lower edge.

How to Sew an Insulated Roman Shade

1) Cut insulated lining and shade fabric as directed in cutting directions (page 61). Splice lining for added length, if necessary, as directed on page 61. Position a 4" (10 cm) channel at lower edge of the shade, 8" (20.5) from cut edge.

2) Pin shade and insulated lining, with right sides together and top and side edges even. The shade fabric will not lie flat because of the 3" (7.5 cm) added for side hems. Stitch ½" (1.3 cm) seams. Zigzag or edgestitch close to cut edge to reduce bulk and prevent insulation from curling.

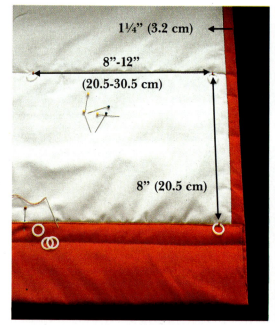

5) Place a 2½" (6.5 cm) strip of magnetic tape on the right side of shade fabric on the seam allowance of lower hem area, just below edge of insulation. If magnetic seal is used on lower edge, firmly press long strip of magnetic tape across shade at lower edge of insulation.

6) Turn shade right side out. Turn under 4" (10 cm) double-fold hem at lower edge. Be sure lower edge is square. Taper side hem edges slightly so they do not show on right side. Stitch close to hem fold; stitch 1" (2.5 cm) from first stitching line to form rod pocket.

7) Place shade, lining side up, on flat surface. Do not press. Mark positions for rings on quilting rows. Place rings 1¼" (3.2 cm) from sides. Space vertical rows 8" to 12" (20.5 to 30.5 cm) apart. Pin through all layers and each ring to prevent shifting. Tack on rings.

3) Place the roll of magnetic tape on newspaper and spray-paint one edge of the roll. This marks the lengthwise polarity. The polarity is important when attaching tape to shade and window. Separate scored lengths of tape or cut 3¼" (8.3 cm) lengths. Round tape corners with scissors to prevent sharp corners from tearing fabric.

4) Position two strips of magnetic tape in each channel, placing strips on the seam allowance on wrong side of shade fabric. Place all strips in the same direction, using painted edges as guide to polarity. Peel off paper backing and press firmly. Do not place magnetic tape in mounting area at top of shade or in lower hem area.

8) Wrap ends of weight rod with tape, or file rough edges to reduce wear on shade fabric. Insert weight rod in rod pocket. Slipstitch opening closed.

9) Attach a plain or lock pulley for first row on the pull side of shade. Pulley supports the additional weight and accommodates more strings than screw eyes do. Attach weighted shade pull. Mount and string shade (page 64).

10) Clean window frame with alcohol to ensure a tight bond. Place long strips of magnetic tape on the sides of the shade to match polarity; mark the top of the strip. Remove strip from shade; peel off backing, and press strip to the window frame.

How to Mount an Insulated Shade Using an Outside Mount

1) Cut 1" × 2" (2.5 × 5 cm) board to the width of finished shade. Wrap shade up and over edge of board; staple to back. Place pulley and screw eyes directly above rows of rings.

2) String as for Roman shade, pages 50 and 51, steps 12 and 13. Screw mounting board into wall. Attach awning cleat to side of window frame or wall if not using a lock pulley.

How to Mount an Insulated Shade Using an Inside Mount

1) Cut 1" × 2" (2.5 × 5 cm) board to fit inside window opening. Wrap shade over edge of board; staple. Place pulley and screw eyes directly above rows of rings. String as for Roman shade, pages 50 and 51, steps 12 and 13.

2) Screw mounting board into top of window frame. Attach awning cleat to side of window frame or wall if not using a lock pulley.

How to Mount an Insulated Shade Using a Hybrid Mount

1) Cut 1" × 2" (2.5 × 5 cm) board to fit inside window opening. Fold shade over at upper edge to finished length. Place fold along upper edge of board so sides of shade extend equally beyond board. Lift shade and staple to mounting board near the fold.

2) Place narrow cardboard strip over stapled portion of shade with upper edge of cardboard even with upper edge of mounting board; staple. String as for Roman shade, pages 50 and 51, steps 12 and 13. Screw mounting board into top of window frame. Attach awning cleat to side of window frame or wall.

Cornices & Valances

A shirred valance (shown above) is a short shirred panel. Install a shirred valance on a separate rod that extends 1" to 2" (2.5 to 5 cm) in front of the curtain rod.

A flat or tailored valance has no extra fullness. This valance is installed on a plain curtain rod, or attached to a 1" × 4" (2.5 × 10 cm) mounting board. Install the mounting board with angle irons to extend beyond the curtain; on Roman shades, attach the valance directly to the mounting board.

Cornices and valances are decorative headings that are mounted above shades, curtains and draperies. Their purpose is to hide exposed rods, plain mountings and tops of conventionally mounted roller shades.

Cornices and valances are usually about one-eighth the curtain or shade length. Make cornices 3" to 4" (7.5 to 10 cm) wider than the window treatment, projecting 2" to 3" (5 to 7.5 cm) in front of it.

Cornices are firm, boxlike structures made from wood, heavy cardboard or foamboard, usually padded and upholstered.

Valances are simple fabric headings. Make them shirred or flat, with plain, trimmed or shaped edges to suit the window treatment.

A padded cornice has a closed top that protects curtains from dust. Cornices also make windows more energy efficient by limiting airflow at the top of the window.

Pleated Draperies

Pleated draperies are easy to sew with pleater tape, which eliminates tedious, complicated measuring.

Pinch pleats are the traditional pleated heading for draperies. Each pinch pleat is actually three small pleats grouped together at regular intervals. Pleater tape for pinch pleats has evenly spaced pockets woven into it; special four-pronged pleater hooks inserted into the pockets draw up the pleats.

Select pleater tape that gives the desired drapery fullness. Some pleater tapes are designed to give an exact double fullness; others allow for more or less than double fullness, depending on how the pockets are used. Determine the drapery fullness (page 27) according to the fabric weight; lightweight fabrics require more fullness than heavy fabrics.

Panel draperies are stationary pleated panels that hang at the sides of the window.

Draw draperies can be closed to cover the entire width of the window. These draperies hang on traverse rods and pull open to one side only (one-way draw) or to both sides (two-way draw).

Before cutting fabric or tape, prepleat the *tape only* using pleater hooks to determine the finished width of the draperies and the pleat position. Pleat tape to the width of the drapery panel and hang it on the rod. Adjust pleats as necessary so the last pleat of the panel is at the corner of the rod return. Do not position pleats on the return or at the center of two-way draperies where panels overlap. Remove pleater hooks and measure tape to determine the finished width of drapery panels, as in steps 1 and 2, opposite.

✂ Cutting Directions

After pleating tape to correct size, cut pleater tape for each panel so that panels have pockets in the same position. Add ½" (1.3 cm) at each end of pleater tape for finishing.

Cut decorator fabric so width is the length of the pleater tape plus 4" (10 cm) to allow for 1" (2.5 cm) double-fold side hems. Seam fabric if necessary, allowing 1" (2.5 cm) for each seam. For length, cut fabric finished length, plus 6½" (16.3 cm) to allow for 3" (7.5 cm) double-fold hem and ½" (1.3 cm) for turning under on upper edge.

YOU WILL NEED

Decorator fabric for draperies.

Pleater tape to match style of heading.

Pleater hooks and end pins.

How to Sew Unlined Pinch-pleated Draperies

1) Prepleat pleater tape to finished width of drapery panel. Leave space unpleated at one end of tape for overlap and at other end for return.

2) Position the pleater tape on installed traverse rod and adjust pleats if necessary. Fold ends under ½" (1.3 cm). Remove hooks. Cut drapery panels using pleater tape as guide.

3) Turn under double-fold hem on lower edge and double-fold hems on sides; stitch. Mark ½" (1.3 cm) from upper edge on right side of drapery.

4) Pin upper edge of pleater tape, pocket side up, along marked line so that pleater tape overlaps drapery ½" (1.3 cm). Stitch ¼" (6 mm) from edge of pleater tape.

5) Fold pleater tape to inside of drapery so it is even with finished upper edge of drapery; press. Stitch lower edge and both sides of tape, following guideline on tape, if marked.

6) Insert hooks. Push prongs all the way up into pleats. Adjust folds between hooks.

Pillow Fashions

Pillow styles range from simple to elaborate. Choice of technique affects your sewing time. Choose a simple knife-edge pillow, or invest more time in tailoring a box pillow complete with cording and a zipper.

1) Neckrolls are small round bolsters that are often trimmed with lace or ruffles. Sleeping bag pillows are the simplest neckroll bolsters to make. They are made with a drawstring closure at each end of a one-piece tube.

2) Shirred corded pillow is made by inserting gathered cording in the seam around the pillow. Cording is gathered using a technique, known as shirring, to gather the bias strip that covers the cord. Make cording in matching or contrasting fabric to add a decorative finish to a pillow.

3) Shirred box pillow uses shirring to gather both edges of the boxing strip. This makes the pillow softer than the traditional box pillow.

4) Flange pillow has a single or double, flat self-border, usually 2" (5 cm) wide, around a plump knife-edge pillow.

5) Mock box pillow is a variation of the knife-edge pillow, with shaped corners to add depth. Corners made using *gathered* style are tied inside the pillow.

6) Ruffled pillow features gathered lace or ruffles made in single or double layers. Pillow tops framed by ruffles in matching or contrasting fabric make attractive showcases for needlepoint, quilting, embroidery or candlewicking.

7) Box pillow has the added depth of a straight or shirred boxing strip. It can be soft for a scatter pillow, or firm for a chair cushion or floor pillow.

8) Mock box pillow can be made with *mitered* corners to create a tailored box shape.

9) Knife-edge pillow is the easiest pillow to make. It consists of two pieces of fabric sewn together, turned right side out and stuffed.

10) Corded pillow is a knife-edge pillow with matching or contrasting cording sewn in the seams. Use purchased cording or make your own. Or finish the pillow with a mock corded edge for a corded look without extra sewing time or fabric. Corded pillows are often called piped pillows.

Pillow Fabrics, Forms & Fillings

To choose the right fabric for your pillow, consider how the pillow will be used and where it will be placed in your home. For a pillow that will receive hard wear, select a sturdy, firmly woven fabric that will retain its shape.

Pillows get their shape from forms or loose fillings. Depending on their washability, loose fillings may be stuffed directly into the pillow covering or encased in a separate liner for easy removal. For ease in laundering or drycleaning, make a separate inner covering or liner for the stuffing, using lightweight muslin or lining fabric, or use purchased pillow forms. Make the liner as you would a knife-edge pillow (pages 72 and 73), fill it with stuffing, and machine-stitch it closed. Choose from several kinds of forms and fillings.

Standard polyester forms are square, round and rectangular for knife-edge pillows in sizes from 10" to 30" (25.5 to 76 cm). These forms are nonallergenic, washable, do not bunch, and may have muslin or polyester outer coverings. Choose muslin-covered forms for pillows with hook and loop tape closings. The loose muslin fibers do not catch on the rough side of the tape.

Polyurethane foam is available in sheets ½" to 5" (1.3 to 12.5 cm) thick for firm pillows and cushions. Some stores carry a high-density foam, 4" (10 cm) thick, for extra firm cushions. Since cutting the foam is difficult, ask the salesperson to cut a piece to the size of your pillow. If you must cut your own foam, use an electric or serrated knife with silicone lubricant sprayed on the blade. Polyurethane foam is also available shredded.

Polyester fiberfill is washable, nonallergenic filling for pillows or pillow liners. Fiberfill comes in loose-pack bags or pressed into batting sheets of varying densities. For a smooth pillow, sew an inner liner of batting, then stuff with loose fill. Soften the hard edges of polyurethane foam by wrapping the form with batting.

Kapok is vegetable fiber filling, favored by some decorators because of its softness. However, kapok is messy to work with and becomes matted with use.

Down is washed, quill-less feathers from the breasts of geese and ducks. Down makes the most luxurious pillows, but it is expensive and not readily available.

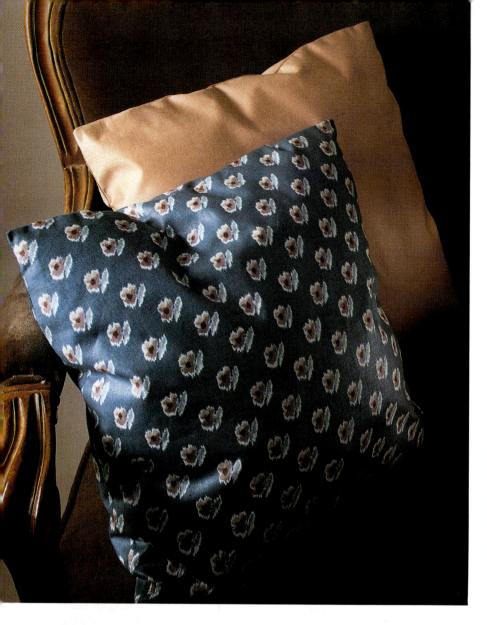

Knife-edge Pillow or Liner

Knife-edge pillows are plump in the center and flat around the edges. These simple pillows can be made in half an hour.

Use the knife-edge pillow directions to make removable pillow liners. Sew liners from muslin, sheeting, cotton sateen or similar fabrics.

✂ Cutting Directions

Cut front and back 1" (2.5 cm) larger than finished pillow or liner. For hook and loop tape or zipper closure, add 1½" (3.8 cm) to back width; for overlap closure, add 5½" (14 cm).

YOU WILL NEED

Decorator fabric for pillow front and back.

Lining fabric for pillow liner, front and back.

Pillow form or polyester fiberfill. Use 8 to 12 oz. (227 to 360 g) fiberfill for a 14" (35.5 cm) pillow, depending on desired firmness.

Zipper or other closure (optional) may be inserted (pages 88 to 91).

How to Make a Knife-edge Pillow or Liner

1) Fold front into fourths. Mark a point halfway between the corner and the fold on each open side. At corner, mark a point ½" (1.3 cm) from each raw edge.

2) Trim from center mark to corner, gradually tapering from the edge to the ½" (1.3 cm) mark. Taper from ½" (1.3 cm) mark to center mark on opposite edge.

3) Unfold front and use it as a pattern for trimming back so that all corners are slightly rounded. This will eliminate dog-ears on the corners of the finished pillow.

4) Pin front to back, right sides together. Stitch ½" (1.3 cm) seam, leaving opening on one side for turning and stuffing. Backstitch at the beginning and end of seam.

5) Trim corners diagonally, ⅛" (3 mm) from stitching. On pillows with curved edges or round corners, clip seam allowance to stitching at intervals along curves.

6) Turn pillow right side out, pulling out corners. Press the seams. Press under the seam allowances in the opening.

7a) Insert a purchased pillow form into the pillow, or stuff the pillow with polyester fiberfill as in step 7b, below. Use a removable form or liner in pillows that will be drycleaned or laundered.

7b) Stuff pillow or liner with polyester fiberfill, gently pulling pieces apart to fluff and separate fibers. Work filling into corners, using long, blunt tool such as a spoon handle.

8) Pin opening closed and edgestitch close to folded edge, backstitching at beginning and end of the stitching. Or slipstitch opening closed.

Corded Knife-edge Pillow

Cording adds stability to pillows and gives them a more tailored look. Cording is made by covering cord with bias strips.

✂ Cutting Directions

Cut pillow front and back 1" (2.5 cm) larger than finished pillow. For hook and loop tape or zipper closure, add 1½" (3.8 cm) to back width; for overlap closure, add 5½" (14 cm). Cut bias strips for cording as in step 1, below.

YOU WILL NEED

Decorator fabric for pillow front, back and cording.

Cord (twisted white cotton or polyester cable), 3" (7.5 cm) longer than distance around pillow.

Pillow form or knife-edge liner.

Zipper or other closure (optional) may be inserted (pages 88 to 91).

How to Make a Corded Knife-edge Pillow

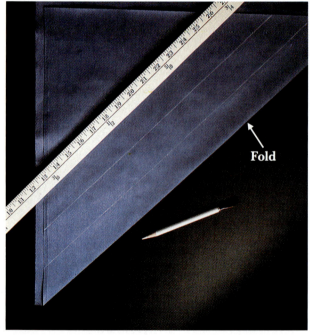

1) Cut bias strips. Determine bias grainline by folding fabric diagonally so selvage aligns with crosswise cut. For ¼" (6 mm) cord, mark and cut 1⅝" (4.2 cm) strips parallel to bias grainline. Cut wider strips for thicker cord.

2) Pin strips at right angles, right sides together, offset slightly **(a)**. Stitch ¼" (6 mm) seams **(b)**, and press open, making one continuous strip equal in length to perimeter of pillow plus 3" (7.5 cm). Trim seam allowances even with edges **(c)**.

3) Center cord on wrong side of bias strip. Fold strip over cord, aligning raw edges. Using zipper foot on right side of needle, stitch close to cord, gently stretching bias to help cording lie smoothly around pillow.

4) Pin the cording to the right side of the pillow front, with raw edges aligned. To ease corners, clip seam allowances to stitching at corners.

5) Stitch, crowding the cord; stop stitching 2" (5 cm) from the point where ends of cording will meet. Leave needle in fabric. Cut off one end of cording so it overlaps the other end by 1" (2.5 cm).

6) Take out 1" (2.5 cm) of stitching from each end of cording. Trim cord ends so they just meet.

7) Fold under ½" (1.3 cm) of overlapping bias strip. Lap it around the other end and finish stitching. Pin pillow front to back, right sides together.

8) Stitch inside stitching line, using zipper foot; crowd stitching against cord. Leave opening. Finish as for knife-edge pillow, page 73, steps 5 to 7b. Slipstitch opening closed.

Mock Box Pillow

Mock box pillows are variations of knife-edge pillows and can be made in three styles. Corners on gathered styles are tied inside the pillow. Mitered styles have a short seam across each corner to create a tailored box shape. Pleated styles have neat tucks at each corner. Pillows with gathers or pleats are sometimes called Turkish pillows.

✄ Cutting Directions

Cut pillow front and back the size of the pillow form plus 1" (2.5 cm) for seams. For hook and loop tape or zipper closure, add 1½" (3.8 cm) to back width; for overlap closure, add 5½" (14 cm).

YOU WILL NEED

Knife-edge pillow form. Or, make a mock box pillow liner using the directions below.

Decorator fabric for pillow front and back.

Zipper or other closure (optional) may be inserted in center back (page 90).

How to Make a Mock Box Pillow with Mitered Corners

1) Stitch as directed on page 73, step 4. Press seams open. Separate front and back at corners. Center seams on each side of corner, on top of each other. Pin through seam.

2) Measure on side seam from corner to half the finished depth; for example, for pillow 3" (7.5 cm) deep, measure 1½" (3.8 cm) from corner. Draw a line perpendicular to the seam.

3) Stitch across corner of pillow on marked line; backstitch at beginning and end. Do not trim seam. Finish pillow as for knife-edge pillow, page 73, steps 6 to 7b. Slipstitch

How to Make a Mock Box Pillow with Gathered Corners

1) Stitch pillow front to pillow back as for knife-edge pillow, page 73, steps 4 and 5. Measure on each seamline from corner to finished pillow depth. Draw diagonal line across the corner.

2) Hand-baste on diagonal line with topstitching and buttonhole twist or doubled thread. Pull up thread to gather.

3) Wrap thread several times around corner; secure with knot. Do not trim corner. Repeat for each corner. Finish as for knife-edge pillow, page 73, steps 6 to 7b. Slipstitch opening closed.

How to Make a Mock Box Pillow with Pleated Corners

1) Fold corner in half diagonally. On raw edge, measure from the corner to half the finished pillow depth plus ½" (1.3 cm); for example, for pillow 3" (7.5 cm) deep, measure 2" (5 cm) from the corner.

2) Mark measured point with ¼" (6 mm) snips through both seam allowances. Fold corner back at snips to form triangle. Mark fold with pin. Press triangle in place.

3) Spread corner flat, right side up. Fold fabric from snip to pin; bring fold to pressed center mark, forming pleat. Pin pleat in place. Repeat for other side.

4) Baste across pleat, ½" (1.3 cm) from raw edge, removing pins as you stitch. Trim triangle-shaped piece from corner. Repeat for each corner of front and back.

5) Pin front to back, right sides together, with front tucked into back to form a "basket." Match pleated corners precisely.

6) Stitch ½" (1.3 cm) seam, leaving opening on one side. Finish as for knife-edge pillow, page 73, steps 6 to 7b. Slipstitch opening closed.

Mock Corded Pillow

Mock corded pillows are corded *after* the pillow is assembled.

✄ Cutting Directions

Cut pillow front 1" (2.5 cm) larger than the finished pillow. Cut back the same length as front. For hook and loop tape or zipper closure, add 1½" (3.8 cm) to back width; for overlap closure, add 5½" (14 cm).

YOU WILL NEED

Decorator fabric for pillow front and back.

Hook and loop tape or zipper, 2" (5 cm) shorter than length of pillow.

Cord, ½" to 1" (1.3 to 2.5 cm), equal in length to distance around the pillow.

Pillow form or knife-edge liner.

How to Make a Mock Corded Pillow

1) **Insert** hook and loop tape or other closure in center of pillow back, pages 88 to 90. Trim corners of front and back into curves.

2) **Pin** front to back, right sides together. Stitch ¼" (6 mm) seam around entire pillow. Turn pillow right side out.

3) **Pin** cord inside pillow, as tightly as possible against seam. Ends of cord should just meet.

4) **Stitch** cord from right side, crowding stitching against cord, using zipper foot. Leave 3" (7.5 cm) opening where cord ends meet.

5) **Pull** out cord about 4" (10 cm) at each end to gather. Adjust gathers. Cut cord so ends just meet. Tack ends together.

6) **Topstitch** opening closed, using zipper foot. Start and end stitching on previous stitching lines. Insert pillow form or liner.

Box Pillow

Box pillows can be used for cushions as well as for casual pillows. They are firm because of the boxing strip that is sewn between the pillow front and back.

✄ Cutting Directions

Cut pillow front and back 1" (2.5 cm) larger than finished pillow. Cut the boxing strip with length equal to distance around pillow plus 1" (2.5 cm) for seams, width equal to depth of pillow plus 1" (2.5 cm).

YOU WILL NEED

Decorator fabric for pillow front, back and boxing strip.

Polyurethane foam wrapped in batting. Or make a box pillow liner, using directions below.

How to Make a Box Pillow

1) Stitch short ends of boxing strip, right sides together, to form continuous loop. Fold loop into fourths and mark each fold with ⅜" (1 cm) clip on both edges.

2) Pin boxing strip to pillow front, right sides together, raw edges even, matching clipped points on strip to pillow corners.

3) Stitch ½" (1.3 cm) seam, shortening stitches for 1" (2.5 cm) on each side of corner; take one or two stitches diagonally across each corner instead of sharp pivot.

4) Pin boxing strip to pillow back, right sides together; match clips to corners. Stitch seam as in step 3, leaving one side open. Press seams, turning under seam allowances at opening. Insert form or liner; slipstitch opening closed.

Ruffled Pillow

Ruffles add interest to a pillow or enhance needlework pillows. Make ruffles from matching or contrasting fabric, or purchase lace or eyelet ruffling.

✂ Cutting Directions

Cut pillow front and back 1" (2.5 cm) larger than finished pillow. Cut ruffle strips twice the desired width plus 1" (2.5 cm) for seam, length two to three times the distance around pillow. Ruffles are usually about 3" (7.5 cm) wide.

YOU WILL NEED

Decorator fabric for pillow front and back and double ruffle.

Purchased ruffling (optional), equal in length to distance around pillow plus 1" (2.5 cm).

Cord, (string, crochet cotton or dental floss) for gathering.

Pillow form or knife-edge liner.

How to Make a Ruffled Pillow

1) **Stitch** short ends of ruffle strip with ½" (1.3 cm) seam, right sides together, to form a loop. Fold strip in half lengthwise, wrong sides together; fold into fourths. Mark each fold with a ⅜" (1 cm) clip.

2) **Prepare** raw edge for gathering by zigzagging over a cord (page 38) or stitching two rows of bastestitching. Match clips on ruffle to corners of pillow front, right sides together and raw edges even. Pin at corners.

3) Pull up the gathering cord until ruffle fits each side of the pillow front. Distribute gathers, allowing extra fullness at corners so ruffle will lie flat in finished pillow. Pin ruffle in place.

4) Machine-baste ruffle to pillow front, stitching just inside gathering row.

5) Pin pillow back to front, right sides together, with ruffle between pieces. Stitch ½" (1.3 cm) seam, leaving 8" (20.5 cm) opening on one side for turning.

6) Turn pillow right side out. Insert pillow form or knife-edge liner; slipstitch opening closed.

Flange Pillows

A *flange* is a flat border around a plump knife-edge pillow. Flanges may be single or double, and are usually about 2" (5 cm) wide. The double-flange pillow is made with a closure; the single-flange pillow is sewn closed.

✂ Cutting Directions

For single flange, cut pillow front and back 5" (12.5 cm) larger than stuffed inner area. This allows for 2" (5 cm) flange and ½" (1.3 cm) seam on each side.

For double flange, cut pillow front 9" (23 cm) larger than pillow form. This allows for a 2" (5 cm) flange and ½" (1.3 cm) seam on each side. For hook and loop tape or zipper closure, add 1½" (3.8 cm) to back width; for overlap closure, add 5½" (14 cm).

YOU WILL NEED

Decorator fabric for pillow front and back.

Polyester fiberfill for single flange pillow, about 6 oz. (170 g) for 12" (30.5 cm) pillow.

Pillow form or knife-edge liner for double flange pillow, to fit inner area.

Zipper or alternate closure for double flange pillow, 2" (5 cm) shorter than length of stuffed inner area (pages 89 and 90).

How to Make a Single-Flange Pillow

1) Pin pillow front to back, right sides together. Stitch ½" (1.3 cm) seam, leaving 8" (20.5 cm) opening. Turn right side out. Press. Topstitch 2" (5 cm) from edge, beginning and ending at opening.

2) Stuff inner area with polyester fiberfill. Work filling into corners, using long blunt tool such as spoon handle. Do not stuff the flange.

3) Topstitch inner area closed, using zipper foot, starting and ending at first stitching line. Slipstitch flange opening, or edgestitch around entire pillow.

How to Make a Double-Flange Pillow with Mitered Corners

1) Insert zipper (page 90), hook and loop tape or snap tape (page 89) in pillow back.

2) Press under 2½" (6.5 cm) on each side of front and back. Place front and back together to make sure corners match; adjust pressed folds if necessary.

3) Open out corner. Fold corner diagonally so pressed folds match (arrows). Press diagonal fold.

4) Open out corner. Fold through center of corner (dotted line), right sides together.

5) Pin on diagonal fold line, raw edges even. Stitch on fold line at right angle to corner fold.

6) Trim seam to ⅜" (1 cm). Press seam open.

7) Turn corner right side out. Use point turner to get a sharp point. Press edges. Repeat with other corners, front and back.

8) Pin pillow front to back, wrong sides together, matching mitered corners carefully.

9) Measure 2" (5 cm) from edge for flange; mark stitching line with transparent tape. Topstitch through all thicknesses along edge of tape. Insert pillow form or liner.

Shirred Pillows

Shirred cording or boxing strips give pillows a formal look.

✂ Cutting Directions

For shirred box pillow, cut pillow front and back 1" (2.5 cm) larger than finished pillow. Cut boxing strip 1" (2.5 cm) wider than depth of form and two to three times longer than distance around form.

For shirred corded pillow, cut pillow front and back 1" (2.5 cm) larger than finished pillow. For cording, cut fabric strips on the crosswise grain, wide enough to cover cord plus 1" (2.5 cm) for seam. The combined length of the strips should be two to three times the distance around pillow.

YOU WILL NEED

Decorator fabric for pillow front and back and for cording or boxing strips.

Cord (twisted white cotton or polyester cable, if making shirred cording). Cut 3" (7.5 cm) longer than distance around pillow.

Gathering cord (string, crochet cotton or dental floss).

Pillow form wrapped in polyester batting, or liner.

How to Make a Shirred Box Pillow

1) Join short ends of boxing strip with ½" (1.3 cm) seam. Prepare raw edges for gathering by zigzagging over cord (page 38) or by stitching two rows of bastestitching. Fold strip into fourths and mark both edges of folds with ⅜" (1 cm) clips.

2) Pin boxing strip to pillow front, right sides together, raw edges even, matching clips on boxing strip to pillow corners. Pull up the gathering cord to fit each side of the pillow.

How to Make Shirred Cording

1) Join ends of cording strips using ¼" (6 mm) seams. Press the seams open. Stitch one end of the cord to the wrong side of the cording strip, ⅜" (1 cm) from the end of the strip.

2) Fold cording strip around cord, wrong sides together, matching raw edges. Using zipper foot, machine-baste for 6" (15 cm), close to but not crowding cord. Stop stitching with needle in fabric.

3) Raise presser foot. While gently pulling cord, push cording strip back to end of cord until fabric behind needle is tightly shirred. Continue stitching in 6" (15 cm) intervals until all cording is shirred.

4) Insert pin through strip and cord at end to secure cord. Distribute gathers evenly. Attach shirred cording to pillow front and join ends of cord, page 75, steps 4 to 8.

3) Distribute gathers evenly, pinning as necessary. Stitch all four sides inside gathering row, stitching corners as directed on page 79, step 3.

4) Pin the lower edge of the boxing strip to pillow back. Repeat steps 2 and 3, except stitch only three sides, leaving one side open to insert the pillow form.

5) Finish as for knife-edge pillow, page 73, steps 6 and 7a, inserting a pillow form wrapped in polyester batting. Slipstitch opening closed.

Neckroll & Sleeping Bag Pillow

Neckrolls and sleeping bag pillows are small, round bolsters with removable covers that gather at the ends with drawstrings.

✂ Cutting Directions

For neckroll, cut fabric same width as circumference of pillow plus 1" (2.5 cm) for seam; length equal to length of pillow plus 1" (2.5 cm). Cut two end strips, the same length as circumference of pillow plus 1" (2.5 cm) for seam; width same as half the diameter of pillow plus 1½" (3.8 cm) for casing.

For sleeping bag pillow, cut fabric same width as circumference of pillow plus 1" (2.5 cm); length equal to length of pillow plus diameter of pillow plus 1½" (3.8 cm) for casing.

YOU WILL NEED

Decorator fabric for tube, and for two end strips if making neckroll.

Ruffled eyelet trim for neckroll. Cut two pieces, each same length as circumference of pillow plus 1" (2.5 cm) for seam.

Ribbon for drawstring, ¼" (6 mm) wide and about 1½ yds. (1.4 m) long. Clip ends diagonally.

Polyester fiberfill batting to form pillow; width same as length of pillow, and about 1 yd. (.95 m) long.

How to Make a Neckroll

1) Roll batting as directed in step 1 for sleeping bag pillow. Fold fabric for tube in half lengthwise, right sides together. Stitch ½" (1.3 cm) seam on lengthwise edge; press seam open.

2) Turn tube right side out. Join ends of each strip of eyelet with French seams. Pin eyelet to each end of tube, with right sides together and edges even. Stitch ¼" (6 mm) seam.

3) Press under ¼" (6 mm), then ½" (1.3 cm) on one long edge of each end strip **(a)** to form casing for ribbon. Open pressed casing **(b)**; stitch short ends of each strip, right sides together. Press seam open.

How to Make a Sleeping Bag Pillow

1) Roll up short side of polyester batting loosely until desired size for pillow. Tack end in place with loose slipstitches.

2) Press under ¼" (6 mm), then ½" (1.3 cm) on each short end of fabric to form casing. Fold fabric in half lengthwise, right sides together. Stitch ½" (1.3 cm) seam; press open.

3) Edgestitch casing for ribbon and finish pillow as directed in steps 5 and 6, below, for neckroll.

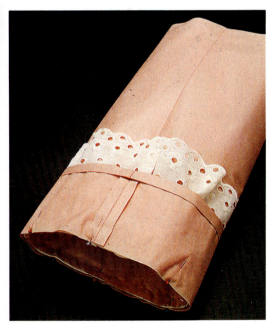

4) Pin unpressed edge of strips to ends of tube, right sides together, with eyelet between tube and strip. Stitch ½" (1.3 cm) seam. If machine has free arm, slip tube over it to stitch circle.

5) Edgestitch close to inside folds of fabric strips, starting and ending at seam. Backstitch to secure the stitching. Clip 3 or 4 stitches on casing seam to make opening for ribbon.

6) Thread ribbon through casings, using safety pin or bodkin. Press seam allowances toward center of pillow; topstitch through all layers. Insert batting. Pull up ribbons and tie.

Pillow Closures

A simple overlap closure is a technique for pillow shams (page 118) as well as an easy and inexpensive closure method for any pillow.

Snap tape and hook and loop tape are easy to handle and give closures a flat, smooth finish. Snap tape allows some give on closures and is suitable for pillows that are very soft. Because closure seam allowances are ¾" (2 cm) wide, use ⅝" (1.5 cm) tape.

Overlap closures are placed in the center back of a pillow. Zippers, hook and loop tape or snap tape can be inserted in the center back or side seam. Except for pillows with overlap closures, cut pillows allowing for ¾" (2 cm) seam allowances on closure seam.

How to Sew an Overlap Closure

1) Cut pillow back 5½" (14 cm) wider than front to allow 3" (7.5 cm) overlap. Cut back in half, cutting *across* widened dimension.

2) Press under ¼" (6 mm), then 1" (2.5 cm) for double-fold hem on each center edge of pillow back. Edgestitch or blindstitch the hems in place.

3) Pin pillow front to back with raw edges even and hemmed edges overlapping in center. Stitch ½" (1.3 cm) seams. Turn right side out and insert pillow form or liner.

How to Sew a Side Seam Closure with Hook and Loop or Snap Tape

1) Prepare seam, page 91, steps 1 and 2. Cut tape 1" (2.5 cm) longer than opening. Trim one seam allowance to ½" (1.3 cm). Place hook side of tape along fold of trimmed seam allowance; ends extend ½" (1.3 cm) beyond opening. Secure with basting tape or pins.

2) Stitch hook side of tape close to edges on all four sides, stitching through pillow back and seam allowance. Stitches show on right side of pillow.

3) Stitch loop side of tape to wrong side of opposite seam allowance, overlapping tape ⅛" (3 mm) on seam allowance, and extending tape ½" (1.3 cm) beyond opening at each end.

4) Turn loop side of tape to right side of seam allowance and stitch to seam allowance on remaining three sides.

5) Place hook side of tape on loop side of tape. Pin pillow front to back along three sides, right sides together. Stitch ½" (1.3 cm) seams. Turn pillow right side out and insert pillow form or liner.

6) Snap tape. Apply as directed in steps 1 to 5 making sure balls and sockets are aligned for smooth closure. Use zipper foot to stitch close to snaps.

How to Insert a Centered Zipper in a Pillow Back

1) Cut pillow back 1½" (3.8 cm) wider than front to allow for a ¾" (2 cm) seam allowance at center back. Use zipper 2" (5 cm) shorter than length of finished pillow back.

2) Fold the pillow back in half lengthwise, right sides together. Press. Center zipper along fold. Snip into fold to mark ends of zipper coil (arrows).

3) Stitch ¾" (2 cm) seam from pillow edge to first snip; backstitch. Machine-baste to ½" (1.3 cm) past second snip. Shorten stitch length; backstitch. Stitch to edge. Cut on fold; press seam open.

4) Open zipper and center it face down between snips with coil on seamline. Pin, or use glue stick or basting tape to hold right side of zipper tape on the right seam allowance. Machine-baste in place.

5) Close zipper, and pin or use glue stick or basting tape to hold the left side of tape to the left seam allowance. Machine-baste in place.

6) Spread pillow flat, right side up. Mark top and bottom of zipper coil with pins. Center ½" (1.3 cm) transparent tape over the seam; topstitch along edges of tape. Tie threads on wrong side of pillow; remove basting.

How to Insert a Lapped Zipper in a Pillow Seam

1) Use zipper 2" (5 cm) shorter than length of finished pillow. Pin pillow front to back along one side, right sides together. Position zipper along pinned seam, leaving equal distance at each edge. Mark ends of zipper coil on seam.

2) Stitch ¾" (2 cm) seam at each end of zipper opening; backstitch at marks. Press under ¾" (2 cm) seam allowances.

3) Open zipper. Place one side face down on seam allowance of pillow front, with zipper coil on seamline. Secure with pins, glue stick or basting tape. Using zipper foot, stitch tape to seam allowance only.

4) Close zipper. Spread pillow flat, right side up. Pin the zipper in place from right side, catching the zipper tape underneath.

5) Place ½" (1.3 cm) transparent tape along seamline as stitching guide. Starting at seamline, stitch across bottom of zipper. Pivot and continue stitching. At top of zipper, pivot and stitch to seamline. Pull threads to wrong side and tie.

6) Open zipper. Turn pillow wrong side out and pin front to back on remaining three sides. Stitch ½" (1.3 cm) seam. Turn pillow right side out, and insert pillow form or liner.

Cushions

A cushion is usually shaped to fit a chair or bench. It has a firm inner core, and is anchored to furniture with a tie or tab. Follow directions for any of the basic knife-edge or box pillows to make a cushion.

Because a cushion needs body, use a 1" (2.5 cm) thick piece of polyurethane wrapped with polyester batting to soften the edges, as a core for the cushion.

✂ Cutting Directions

For knife-edge cushion, cut front and back same size as area to be covered adding half the cushion depth and ½" (1.3 cm) for seams to each of the dimensions.

For box cushion, cut boxing strip desired width plus 1" (2.5 cm); cut front and back same size as area to be covered, adding 1" (2.5 cm) to each dimension for cushion fullness and ½" (1.3 cm) for seams.

How to Cut Fabric for Cushions

1) **Measure** length and width of area to be covered by cushion. For a square or rectangular cushion, use these dimensions to cut fabric. For a cushion with unusual shape, prepare a paper pattern.

2) **Cut** paper pattern in same shape as area to be covered. Mark the paper pattern to show where ties or tabs should be attached.

3) **Use** paper pattern to cut fabric for cushion, adding amount for depth and seams for cushion style. Transfer tie or tab markings to edge of right side of fabric.

Tufted Cushion

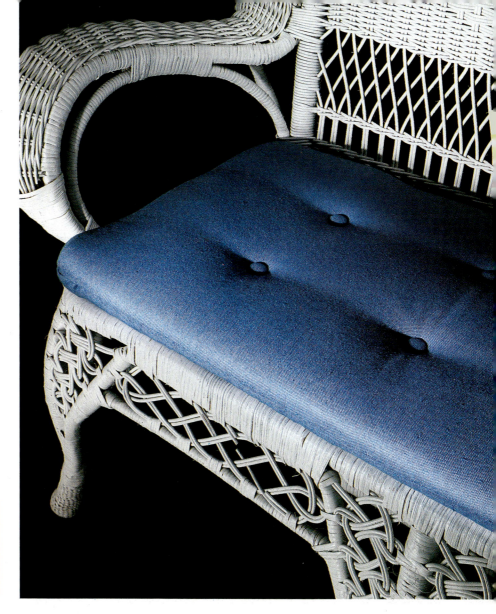

Add button tufting to chair or bench cushions to prevent filling from shifting inside the cover. Tufting is done after the cushion is finished. Tufted cushion covers are usually not removed, so zippers or other closures are not necessary.

Use covered flat buttons with a shank. Buttons for covering are available in kits, complete with a button front and back, and tools that simplify covering the button. Dampen the button fabric just before beginning. As the fabric dries around the button, it will shrink slightly to fit smoothly.

YOU WILL NEED

Long needle, with large eye.

Strong thread such as button and carpet thread or buttonhole twist.

Flat dressmaker buttons with shanks, two for each tuft.

How to Tuft a Cushion

1) Thread a long needle with extra-strong button and carpet thread or several strands of buttonhole twist. Thread strands through button shank; tie ends to shank with double knot.

2) Push needle through cushion, pulling button tight against pillow to create a "dimple." Clip thread near needle.

3) Thread second button on one strand of thread. Tie single knot with both strands and pull until button is tight against bottom of cushion. Wrap thread two or three times around button shank. Tie double knot. Trim threads.

Cushion Ties

Attach cushions to chairs with traditional fabric ties. Ties prevent cushions from sliding, and add a decorative accent to chairs.

Make ties to suit the style of the chair and cushion. Experiment with different sized fabric strips tied around the chair posts, to determine the appropriate length and width of the ties. Trim the fabric strip to desired size to use as a pattern.

✄ Cutting Directions

Cut each tie 1½" (3.8 cm) longer and 1" (2.5 cm) wider than the fabric pattern, allowing ½" (1.3 cm) for seam end and 1" (2.5 cm) for knotting the finished end. Cut two ties for each post where the ties will be attached.

How to Make Cushion Ties

1) Make two ties for each post where ties will be attached. Press under ¼" (6 mm) on long edges of each tie. Press tie in half lengthwise, wrong sides together, pressed edges even; pin.

2) Edgestitch along open edge of ties. Leave both ends of tie open. Tie a single knot at one end of tie, enclosing the raw edges in the knot.

3) Pin unfinished ends of ties to right side of cushion front at marks. Pin cushion front to back, right sides together. Stitch, backstitching over ties. Finish cushion and tie to chair post.

Hook and Loop Tabs

Hook and loop tape tabs make a cushion extremely easy to attach and remove, and because they are small and inconspicuous they blend in well with furniture.

The length of the tab depends on the size of the rung or post that the tab goes around. Measure accurately because the tabs must fit snugly. Tabs may be hand-stitched to existing cushions because they do not need to be stitched in a seam.

✂ Cutting Directions

Cut tabs just long enough to go around chair post and overlap by 1" to 1½" (2.5 to 3.8 cm), plus ½" (1.3 cm) for seam; twice the finished width, plus ½" (1.3 cm).

Cut hook and loop tape 1" to 1½" (2.5 to 3.8 cm) long for each tab.

How to Make Cushion Ties with Hook and Loop Tape

1) Make one tab for each corner. Press under ¼" (6 mm) on each edge of tab. Press tab in half lengthwise, wrong sides together. Edgestitch all four sides of tab.

2) Cut hook and loop tape for each tab. Separate hook and loop sides. Attach opposite sides of tape to opposite sides of tab. Stitch around all four sides of hook and loop tape.

3) Stitch pillow front to back. Before stuffing, pin center of tab to seam at cushion corners. Place all tabs in same direction; stitch and backstitch.

4) Finish cushion. Attach cushion to chair or bench by fastening hook and loop tabs around posts, overlapping ends to secure.

Tables

Tabletop Fashions

Customized tabletop fashions are a simple way to change the look of a room without spending too much time or money. These easy projects make good home sewing sense for several reasons.

Home-sewn table fashions, unlike purchased ones, are not limited to a small selection of standard sizes. Design a tablecloth yourself, and scale it to the exact size and shape of your table. Choose from an abundant supply of fabric colors, patterns and textures to complement the decor of your room.

Because most tablecloths are wider than one fabric width, you must seam fabric widths together to make the tablecloth the width you need. Avoid a center seam by using a full fabric width in the center and stitching narrower side panels to it.

Use selvage edges in seams to eliminate seam finishing. If the selvage tends to pucker, clip it at regular intervals of 1" to 6" (2.5 to 15 cm). If selvages are not used in seams, finish with French or overedge seams. Use plain seams for reversible tablecloths.

Placemats, napkins and table runners give you an opportunity to experiment with finishing techniques you may be reluctant to try on larger projects.

Selecting Fabrics

When you design tabletop fashions, look for durable, stain-resistant fabrics that have been treated to repel soil and water. Permanent press fabrics offer easy care. Drape the fabric over your arm to see how it hangs.

For everyday use, lightweight cotton is appropriate; use a lightweight tablecloth with a table pad to protect fine wood tables. For an elegant look, use a sheer lace or eyelet tablecloth over a heavier cloth.

Small random prints are easier to work with than prints that may need matching. Avoid heavily napped fabrics or fabrics with difficult-to-match design motifs such as printed plaids or stripes, diagonals or one-way patterns.

Measuring the Table

The length of the tablecloth from the edge of the table to the bottom of the cloth is the *drop*. Always include the drop length in your tablecloth measurements.

There are three common drop lengths: short, 10" to 12" (25.5 to 30.5 cm); mid-length, 16" to 24" (40.5 to 61 cm); and floor-length, 28" to 29" (71 to 73.5 cm). Short cloths end at about chair seat height and are good tablecloths for everyday use. Mid-length cloths are more formal. Elegant floor-length coverings are used for buffet and decorator tables.

Round tablecloth. Measure the diameter of the table, then determine the drop length of the cloth. The size of the tablecloth is the diameter of the table plus twice the drop length plus 1" (2.5 cm) for a narrow hem allowance. A narrow hem is the easiest way to finish the curved edge of a round tablecloth.

Square tablecloth. Measure the width of the tabletop; then determine the drop length of the cloth. Add twice the drop length plus 1" (2.5 cm) for a narrow hem allowance or 2½" (6.5 cm) for a wide hem allowance.

Rectangular tablecloth. Measure the length and width of the tabletop, then determine the drop length of the cloth. The size of the finished tablecloth is the width of the tabletop plus twice the drop length, and the length of the tabletop plus twice the drop length. Add 1" (2.5 cm) for a narrow hem or 2½" (6.5 cm) for a wide hem.

Oval tablecloth. Measure the length and width of the tabletop, then determine the drop length of the cloth. Join fabric widths as necessary to make a rectangular cloth the length of the tabletop plus twice the drop length, and the width of the tabletop plus twice the drop length; add 1" (2.5 cm) to each dimension for a narrow hem allowance. Put a narrow hem in an oval tablecloth because it is the simplest way to finish the curved edge. Because oval tables vary in shape, mark the finished size with the fabric on the table. Place weights on the table to hold fabric in place, then use a hem marker or cardboard gauge to mark the drop length evenly.

Round Tablecloths

To determine the yardage for a tablecloth without a flounce, divide tablecloth diameter by fabric width less 1" (2.5 cm). Count fractions as one width. This is the number of widths. Then multiply number of widths by diameter and divide by 36" (100 cm) to find the total yards (meters).

For center of flounced-edge tablecloth, subtract two times the finished depth of the flounce from the finished length of the tablecloth. Determine yardage for center as for tablecloth above.

Determine the flounce length by multiplying diameter of center by 3½; double this figure. For number of strips, divide flounce length by fabric width. Then multiply number of strips by cut depth and divide by 36 for total yards (meters).

✂ Cutting Directions

For tablecloth without a flounce, cut center panel with length equal to tablecloth diameter plus hems. Add partial panels to form square.

For tablecloth with flounce, cut center panel with length equal to the diameter of center plus seam allowances. Add partial panels to form square. Cut strips for flounce the depth of flounce, plus hem and seam allowances and length as determined above.

How to Cut a Round Tablecloth

1) Join fabric panels, right sides together, with ½" (1.3 cm) seams to form square. Fold square into fourths. Pin layers together to prevent slipping.

2) Measure a string the length of the radius of the cloth. Tie one end of string around a marking pencil; pin other end at center folded corner of cloth. Mark outer edge of circle, using string and pencil as compass. Cut on marked line; remove pins.

How to Sew Narrow & Flounced Hems

Narrow hem. Stitch around tablecloth ¼" (6 mm) from edge. Press under on stitching line. Press under ¼" (6 mm) again, easing fullness around curves. Edgestitch close to folded edge. Or, use narrow hemmer.

Flounced edge. Seam strips of flounce, right sides together, to form loop. Hem lower edge. Zigzag over cord to make ruffles (page 38). Attach flounce to tablecloth as for ruffled curtains (page 39).

How to Sew a Corded Hem

1) Multiply diameter of the tablecloth by 3½ to determine length of cording needed. Cut and join bias strips, right sides together, to cover cording (page 74).

2) Cover cording and attach to right side of cloth as for corded pillow, page 75, steps 3 to 7. Zigzag seam and press to back of tablecloth. Topstitch ¼" (6 mm) from cording seam.

How to Sew a Reversible Round Tablecloth

1) Join lining panels, leaving 12" (30.5 cm) opening in one seam for turning. Stitch the lining to the outer tablecloth, wrong sides together, ½" (1.3 cm) from edge. Trim seam or clip curves.

2) Turn tablecloth right side out by pulling outer fabric through opening in lining seam. Slipstitch opening closed.

3) Topstitch ¼" (6 mm) from edge. If lining is contrasting color, match upper thread to outer fabric, bobbin thread to lining.

Square & Rectangular Tablecloths

Make tablecloths the desired width by joining fabric widths as necessary, using full widths in the center and partial widths on the lengthwise edges. Straighten the crosswise ends of fabric (page 28) to square the corners. Use French or overedge seams, or use selvage edges to eliminate seam finishing.

Select the width and finish of the hem to complement the weight and texture of the fabric. Mitering is the neatest way to square corners because it covers raw edges and eliminates bulk.

Determine the amount of fabric needed for the tablecloth by dividing the total width of the tablecloth by the width of your fabric, less 1" (2.5 cm). Multiply this figure, which is the number of panels needed, by the total length of the tablecloth. Divide this number by 36" (100 cm) to get the total yards (meters) required.

Wide and Narrow Hems

1) Wide hem. Press under ¼" to ½" (6 mm to 1.3 cm), then press under 1" or 2" (2.5 or 5 cm) hem on all sides.

2) Open out corner, leaving first fold turned under. Miter corners as for double-flange pillow, page 83, steps 3 to 7. Blindstitch or straight-stitch hem.

Narrow hem. Press under ½" (1.3 cm) on each side. Open corner; fold diagonally so pressed folds match. Press; trim corner. Fold raw edge under ¼" (6 mm). Fold again on first fold line; press. Stitch hem.

Quilted Table Covers

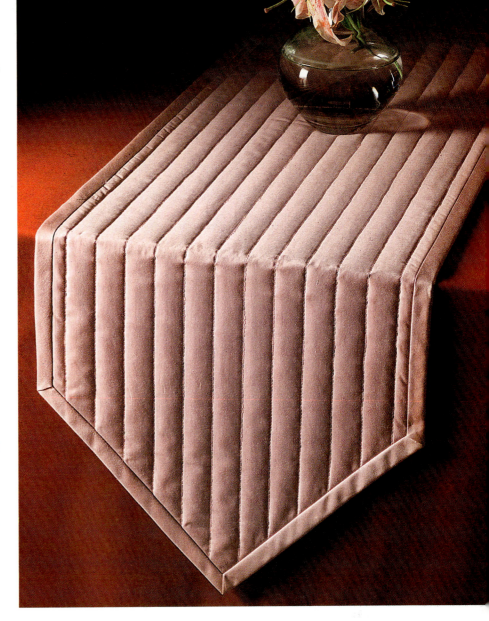

Quilting adds body to table coverings and provides additional protection for table surfaces. The thickness and slight puffiness of quilted table accessories also adds visual appeal. Use quilted fabrics for placemats, table runners and table mats. Finish edges with bias binding (page 105).

Prequilted fabrics are available, but quilting your own fabric provides the luxury of coordinating colors and prints, and the economy of making only the amount of quilted fabric needed for a project. The quilting guide foot with the attached guide bar makes the channel-quilting process easy. Lengthen the stitch length and loosen the pressure for even quilting. Begin by stitching the center quilting row, and work toward the sides.

Use polyester fleece or needle-punched batting for tabletop fashions. It will retain its shape and body when laundered.

How to Machine Quilt Fabric Using a Quilter Bar

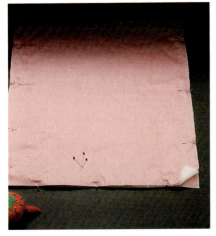

1) Cut fabric, fleece and lining slightly larger than finished size of item. Place fleece between wrong sides of fabric and lining. Pin or baste all three layers together.

2) Mark first quilting line in center of fabric with yardstick and chalk pencil. (If not using quilter bar, mark every quilting row an equal distance apart.)

3) Stitch center line. Determine the distance to next quilting line. Adjust quilter bar to follow the previous row of stitching as you stitch the next row.

Placemats, Table Runners & Table Mats

Placemats, table runners and table mats protect tabletops and add color and style to table settings. Use them over tablecloths, or alone to show off the beauty of wood and glass tables. The sewing techniques for placemats, table runners and table mats are very similar.

Select fabric for mats and runners according to the general guidelines for choosing tablecloth fabrics. Fabric may be machine quilted using the procedure described on page 103.

Finish edges of tabletop projects with wide banding (pages 106 and 107) or bias binding. To make bias binding, cut and join bias strips (page 74). Fold strip in half lengthwise, wrong sides together, and press. Open binding and press cut edges toward center.

Tips for Binding Placemat Edges

Quilted fabrics. Before applying binding, stitch placemat ¼" (6 mm) from edge. Trim batting from hem area to reduce bulk in bound edge.

Slipstitched edges. Open out bias binding. Pin right side of binding to front of mat, raw edges even. Stitch on foldline. Turn binding to back of mat and slipstitch.

Topstitched edges. Open out bias binding. Pin right side of binding to back of mat, raw edges even. Stitch on foldline. Turn binding to front of mat and topstitch.

Placemats can be lined, underlined with fusible interfacing, made of quilted fabric, or sewn double for extra body. Two common finished sizes of placemats are 18" × 12" (46 × 30.5 cm) and 16" × 14" (40.5 × 35.5 cm). Choose the best size for your table and place settings.

Table runners are usually 12" to 18" (30.5 to 46 cm) wide; make them wider if they will be used as placemats. Drop lengths vary from 8" to 12" (20.5 to 30.5 cm). Table runners may be cut on either the lengthwise or the crosswise grain of the fabric, but less piecing of fabric is required if they are cut on lengthwise grain.

Table mats protect the surface of a table without hiding the legs or base. Cut and sew a mat to the exact size of the tabletop and finish the edges.

Square corners. Start at center of edge; fold binding over edge. Stitch to corner. Pin binding to next edge, folding diagonally at corner. Begin stitching at miter. Finish ends, right.

Oval mats. Shape corners of mat using a dinner plate as a guide. Before applying bias binding, shape binding to curves with a steam iron.

Finishing ends. Cut bias binding 1" (2.5 cm) beyond the end. Turn under ½" (1.3 cm); finish stitching to end of binding. Slipstitch.

Banded Placemats

Wide double banding creates reversible placemat.

✂ Cutting Directions

Determine size of finished mat (page 104) and desired width of finished banding. Cut placemat center the size of finished mat minus two times the width of finished banding, plus ½" (1.3 cm). For each mat, cut two centers. Stitch centers, wrong sides together, a scant ¼" (6 mm) from raw edge.

Cut banding twice the finished width plus ½" (1.3 cm); length the distance around outer edge of *finished* mat plus ½" (1.3 cm). Use ¼" (6 mm) seams. Press under ¼" (6 mm) on lengthwise edges. Press in half lengthwise, wrong sides together.

How to Sew Banded Placemats with Mitered Corners

1) Mark beginning stitching point on band the width of finished band plus ¼" (6 mm). Place mark ¼" (6 mm) from corner of mat, raw edges even and right sides together.

2) Mark and pin band at adjacent corner ¼" (6 mm) from edge. Pin between corners. Stitch on foldline from mark to mark; backstitch at ends to secure.

3) Fold band from mat diagonally. Mark out from corner stitching the width of finished band. Fold at mark, right sides together. Mark ¼" (6 mm) from corner of mat.

4) Repeat steps 2 and 3, above, for next two corners.

5) Measure width of finished band from stitching; mark. Mark and stitch as shown. Press seam open; trim. Fold band to reverse side, forming miters.

6) Fold band diagonally to miter corners on reverse side. Pin folded edge of band to stitching line. Slipstitch the mitered corners and edges of band in place.

Trimmed Placemats

Trimmed placemats have banding stitched to one side. Purchase finished trim or cut trim from fabric. The same method may also be used to stitch banding on tablecloths (pages 96 and 97).

✄ Cutting Directions

Cut the placemat 1" (2.5 cm) larger than desired finished size (page 104). Press ½" (1.3 cm) seam allowance to right side of placemat on all edges. Cut trimming long enough to go around edge of placemat, plus 1" (2.5 cm). You will need approximately 61" (155 cm) for each placemat. If making your own banding from fabric, allow ¼" (6 mm) on each side for finishing. Press under ¼" (6 mm) on long sides of banding.

How to Sew Placemats with Mitered Ribbon Trimming

1) Position short end of band ½" (1.3 cm) beyond edge of mat, aligning lengthwise edge of band with folded outer edge of the placemat; pin.

2) Fold trimming straight back at corner so fold is even with edge of mat. Fold trimming diagonally to form right angle; press and pin. Repeat at next two corners.

3) Fold end diagonally at first corner to form right angle; press. Remove pins. Baste on diagonal foldlines, using pins or glue stick.

4) Stitch each corner of trim on diagonal foldline, stitching on wrong side and beginning at inner edge. Backstitch at beginning and end of seam to secure.

5) Adjust mat size or miters if necessary. Trim seam allowances of miters to ¼" (6 mm); press seams open. Press under seam allowance that extends at one corner.

6) Baste trim to mat, with outer edges even. Stitch outer edge, beginning at one side and pivoting at corners; backstitch. Stitch inner edge.

Six Ways to Make and Hem Napkins

Satin stitch. Turn under ½" (1.3 cm) on all sides. Miter corners (page 102). Edgestitch along raw edge to use as guide. Use wide, closely spaced zigzag to stitch from right side over edgestitching.

Zigzag overedge. Trim loose threads from napkin edges. Stitch over raw edge, using wide, closely spaced zigzag. Use overedge foot or special-purpose foot to maintain zigzag width.

Decorative stitch. Press under ¼" (6 mm) and stitch. From right side, stitch with a decorative stitch, using straight stitching as the guideline. Blanket stitch (shown above) gives a hemstitched look.

Napkins

Coordinating napkins are the finishing touch to your tabletop fashions. Standard finished napkins are 14" or 17" (35.5 or 43 cm) square. Before cutting the fabric, square the ends, using a carpenter's square. For fringed napkins, square the ends by pulling a thread (page 28).

Napkin hems can be decorative. Experiment with some of the decorative stitches on your sewing machine. The hemming techniques shown here can also be used on tablecloths and placemats.

✄ Cutting Directions

Cut napkins 1" (2.5 cm) larger than finished size. One yard (meter) of 36" (91.5 cm) wide fabric yields four 17" (43 cm) napkins. A piece of fabric 45" (115 cm) square yields nine 14" (35.5 cm) napkins.

Narrow hem. Press under ¼" (6 mm) double-fold hem on opposite sides of all napkins. Edgestitch from one napkin to the next using continuous stitching. Repeat for remaining sides.

Double-fold hem. Turn under ¼" (6 mm) on all edges and press. Turn under another ¼" (6 mm). Miter corners as directed for narrow hem (page 102). Edgestitch close to folded edge.

Fringe. Cut napkins on a pulled thread to straighten edges. Stitch ½" (1.3 cm) from raw edges with short straight stitches or narrow, closely spaced zigzag. Pull out threads up to the stitching line.

Bed Fashions

Custom-made bed fashions such as comforters, comforter covers, pillow shams and dust ruffles can be ruffled or tailored to suit the decor. Chintzes, polished cottons and sateens are good choices for most bed coverings. Sheets are another practical fabric choice; their width makes seaming unnecessary on comforters and covers.

Permanent press fabrics with soil-resistant finishes are advisable in a child's room. Select fabrics that will launder well without fading.

Comforters are a useful alternative to bedspreads. Make them reversible to change their look, and fill them with polyester batting as flat or as puffy as you wish. Decorator fabrics used for comforters should be pieced together with a full fabric width in the center of the comforter and a partial width on each side.

Comforter covers, also known as *duvet covers,* are removable for easy care. They protect new comforters, salvage worn ones, and quickly change the look of a comforter. They also eliminate the need for a top sheet and blanket on the bed.

Pillow shams are removable, decorative pillow covers. Make pillow shams plain or flanged, ruffled or trimmed, in matching or contrasting fabrics to complement the comforter and dust ruffle. Traditional pillowcases may also be trimmed with ruffles and used as pillow shams.

Dust ruffles or bed skirts are used with comforters. They may be gathered or pleated. Make them in one piece for beds that do not have a footboard. Make them in three pieces for beds that do have a footboard. Attach dust ruffles to a fitted sheet placed over the box spring or to a muslin *deck,* a piece of fabric which fits between the mattress and the box spring.

Fabrics for dust ruffles should be considered for their weight and draping quality, as well as suitability for the style of the dust ruffle or bed skirt.

Measuring the Bed

Measure accurately to make a comforter and dust ruffle that fits the bed perfectly.

Comforters reach 3" to 4" (7.5 to 10 cm) below the mattress line. They have a *drop length* (the distance from the upper edge of the mattress to the bottom of the comforter) of 9" to 12" (23 to 30.5 cm), depending on the depth of the mattress. Determine the drop length by measuring from the top of the mattress to the top of the box spring, then adding to that figure the amount of overlap desired. Take into account fabric stiffness which may cause the comforter to stand away from the side of the bed.

To determine finished comforter size, measure from side to side across the top of the mattress for width, and from the head to the foot of the bed for length. Add the desired drop length to the length of the

bed, and twice the drop length to the width of the bed for finished measurements.

Batting for comforters is available in standard widths for beds of standard sizes; select the proper size for your comforter.

For the finished dust ruffle length, measure from the top of the box spring to the floor; for the deck, measure the width and length of the box spring.

Pillow sizes are 20" × 26" (51 × 66 cm) standard; 20" × 30" (51 × 76 cm) queen; and 20" × 40" (51 × 102 cm) king. Pillow puffiness varies, however, so make the best-fitting shams by measuring the width and length of the pillow with a tape measure across the center of the pillow. Ruffled shams made from lightweight fabrics will droop around the edges if they are cut too large.

Comforter

Comforters have the look of quilts but do not require time-consuming and intricate hand-quilting. They should reach just below the mattress line and be used with dust ruffles or bed skirts.

Comforters are made from three layers: a backing or lining, a bonded polyester batting for warmth and body, and a top layer of decorator fabric.

Because the bulk of the comforter makes machine-quilting difficult to manage, it should be hand-tufted. Tufting, or hand-tied yarn, holds the layers together and emphasizes the appealing puffiness. Place tufts 6" to 10" (15 to 25.5 cm) apart; the design of the fabric may dictate their placement.

✂ Cutting Directions

Cut and seam fabric for comforter top equal to finished size. Cut lining 8" (20.5 cm) larger than finished size for self-binding edge. Or cut lining same as top; finish edge with wide bias binding strips as for quilted placemats (page 105).

YOU WILL NEED

Decorator fabric for comforter.

Lining for comforter.

Bonded polyester batting, proper size for bed width and cut to finished size of comforter.

Yarn, pearl cotton or embroidery floss for tufting, washable if comforter will be laundered.

How to Sew and Tuft a Comforter

1) Place lining face down on flat surface. Leaving 4" (10 cm) border, place batting on lining, then decorator fabric, right side up, edges even with batting.

2) Pin three layers together. Hand-baste layers together with long stitches in parallel rows 8" to 10" (20.5 to 25.5 cm) apart, so layers do not slip.

3) Fold lining to edge of batting. Fold corners diagonally, then fold lining again over front of comforter to form 2" (5 cm) border. Pin in place. Slipstitch binding to comforter along folded edge.

1½" (3.8 cm)

4) Mark positions for tufts. Thread a large needle with double strand of yarn. Working from right side of comforter, make a ¼" (6 mm) stitch through all layers. Leave 1½" (3.8 cm) tail of yarn.

5) Hold all four strands of yarn in one hand, close to comforter. Bring needle behind four strands and over two strands to form loop.

6) Draw needle through loop. Pull ends to secure knot. Clip ends of yarn to ¾" (2 cm).

Comforter Cover

Change the look of a bed with a covered comforter. It can replace a top sheet and blanket, and the removable cover of the comforter makes laundering easy. Sew your own comforter, or use a purchased one of down or of polyester batting.

Choose a washable, lightweight, firmly woven fabric for the cover. Sheets are good fabric choices because they do not require piecing. Seam decorator fabrics together by using a full fabric width in the center of the cover, with partial widths along the sides.

Leave a 36" (91.5 cm) opening in the back of the cover for inserting the comforter. Place the opening about 16" (40.5 cm) from the lower edge on the inside of the cover so it will not show at the ends. Use an overlap, snap tape, hook and loop tape, a zipper or buttons for closure.

✂ Cutting Directions

Cut the front of the cover 1" (2.5 cm) larger than the comforter. Cut the back of the cover according to the closure method you choose. For button closures, add 5½" (14 cm) to back length. For a snap tape, hook and loop or zipper closure, add 1½" (3.8 cm) to back length.

Cut four small fabric strips for tabs, each about 2" (5 cm) square.

YOU WILL NEED

Decorator fabric or sheets for cover, and small amount of extra fabric for tabs.

Snap tape, hook and loop tape, zipper or buttons.

Gripper snaps to hold comforter in place.

How to Sew a Comforter Cover

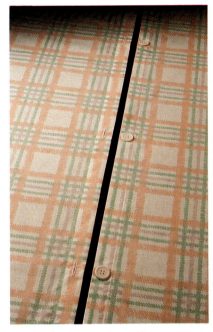

1) Press under 16" (40.5 cm) across the lower edge of the back, right sides together. If using tapes or zipper, snip the fold to mark ends of closure. Stitch ¾" (2 cm) from the fold; backstitch at snips and bastestitch across the closure area. Cut on fold; press seam open.

2a) Insert hook and loop tape (**a**), snap tape (**b**) or zipper (**c**) according to instructions for pillow closures (pages 89 to 91).

2b) Cut back apart on 16" (40.5 cm) fold line for button closure. Press under ¼" (6 mm) then 1" (2.5 cm) hem on each edge; stitch. On hem of shorter piece, make buttonholes 10" to 12" (25.5 to 30.5 cm) apart; attach buttons opposite buttonholes.

3) Pin cover front to cover back, right sides together. For button closure, pin the shorter piece first, lapping the longer piece over it.

4) Make tabs, page 95, step 1. Attach socket side of snaps to tabs, and ball sides to corners of the comforter. Pin a tab at each corner of the cover, edges even.

5) Stitch front and back of cover together with ½" (1.3 cm) seam. Diagonally trim bulk from corners. Turn cover right side out. Insert comforter; snap cover to comforter at corners.

Pillow Shams

Pillow shams can be plain, ruffled or trimmed with a flange or banding. A sham has an overlap, or flap pocket closure, on the back to make it easy to slip a pillow into it. The easiest sham to make is cut in one piece with the ends turned under and hemmed so that the overlap is part of the fold.

To add a ruffle or coordinating flange, cut the front, back and overlap pieces separately so that there will be a seam completely around the pillow. Seams on shams should be finished. Use French seams on one-piece shams and pillowcase shams; zigzag the seams on ruffled shams. Flanged shams have enclosed seams.

✄ Cutting Directions

For one-piece sham, cut fabric same width as pillow plus 1" (2.5 cm); length equal to two times the length of pillow plus 11" (28 cm).

For ruffled sham, cut front and back 1" (2.5 cm) larger than pillow. Cut overlap 10" (25.5 cm) wide, length equal to width of pillow plus 1" (2.5 cm). Cut ruffle two times desired width plus 1" (2.5 cm), and length equal to two times the distance around pillow, plus 1" (2.5 cm).

For flanged pillow sham, cut front 5" (12.5 cm) wider and 5" (12.5 cm) longer than pillow. Cut back 5" (12.5 cm) wider and 2" (5 cm) longer than pillow. Cut overlap 5" (12.5 cm) wider than pillow and 13" (33 cm) long. This allows for ½" (1.3 cm) seams and 2" (5 cm) flange. Cut banding or trimming desired width and long enough to go around entire pillow.

For ruffled pillowcase sham, cut fabric same width as pillow plus 1" (2.5 cm); length equal to two times the length of pillow plus 1" (2.5 cm). Cut ruffle two times desired width plus 1" (2.5 cm), and length four times width of pillow. Cut facing strip 3" (7.5 cm) wide; length equal to two times the width of pillow plus 1" (2.5 cm).

How to Sew a One-piece Sham

1) Stitch ½" (1.3 cm) double-fold hem at one short end. Turn under ½" (1.3 cm), then 2" (5 cm) at the other end; stitch. For overlap, press under 7½" (19.3 cm) on end with wider hem. Fold the sham crosswise, *wrong* sides together, so narrow hemmed edge is in pressed fold. Fold the overlap over the hemmed edge.

2) Stitch ¼" (6 mm) seam on two long sides. Trim seams to ⅛" (3 mm). Turn sham wrong side out. Press seam edges. Stitch ¼" (6 mm) from the edges for French seams. Turn the sham right side out. Insert the pillow.

How to Sew a Ruffled Sham

1) Stitch ½" (1.3 cm) double-fold hem on one short end of sham back. Turn under ½" (1.3 cm), then 2" (5 cm) hem on one long edge of overlap; stitch. Prepare and attach ruffle to right side of sham front, as for ruffled pillow, pages 80 and 81, steps 1 to 4.

2) Pin unfinished edge of overlap to one end of front, right sides together, with ruffle between two layers. Pin back to front, positioning back and overlap as shown. Stitch ½" (1.3 cm) seam around sham. Trim corners; finish seam allowances. Turn right side out and insert pillow.

How to Sew a Flanged Pillow Sham

1) Position banding to front of pillow sham 2½" (6.3 cm) from edge. Miter corners, as for placemats with mitered ribbon trimming, page 107. Stitch *inner* edge of band only.

2) Make sham following instructions for ruffled sham (page 119), omitting ruffle; finish seams. Turn sham right side out and topstitch along outer edge of banding. Insert pillow.

How to Sew a Ruffled Pillowcase Sham

1) Fold sham crosswise, wrong sides together; stitch French seams (page 17). Prepare and attach the ruffle to right side of open end of sham, as directed, pages 80 and 81, steps 1 to 4.

2) Press under ½" (1.3 cm) on one long side of facing strip. Join short ends of strip. Pin right side of strip to right side of pillow sham with ruffle between two fabric layers. Stitch ½" (1.3 cm) seam.

3) Press seam toward pillow sham. Edgestitch or slipstitch along pressed fold of facing strip. (Facing strip is shown in contrasting color to make it more visible.)

Dust Ruffles & Bed Skirts

Dust ruffles and bed skirts are designed to hide the box spring and legs of a bed. They can be made to coordinate with a comforter or quilt. Gathered dust ruffles give a soft effect; pleated bed skirts are more tailored. Dust ruffles and bed skirts are gathered or pleated around only three sides of the bed.

Gathered dust ruffles can be made with either one or two layers of gathered fabric. When making a two-layered dust ruffle, gather the two layers as one piece. The type of fabric you choose determines the fullness of a gathered dust ruffle. Allow three times the fullness for lightweight fabrics; allow two to three times the fullness for mediumweight fabrics.

The directions that follow are for a gathered dust ruffle with split corners; the dust ruffle is attached to a fitted sheet. This open-cornered style, which is made in three sections, is suitable for a bed with a footboard. Dust ruffles may also be made in one continuous piece for beds without footboards.

Pleated bed skirts have deep pleats and they are made from medium to heavyweight fabrics. The directions that follow allow for a 6" (15 cm) pleat at each end corner and the center of each side. A 1" (2.5 cm) double-fold hem is used at the lower edge and sides of the skirt. The pleated bed skirt is for a bed without a footboard; the skirt is attached to a deck. The deck can be made from muslin or from broadcloth or a flat sheet in a color that matches the bed skirt.

✂ Cutting Directions

For gathered dust ruffle length, cut two pieces each the length of the box spring times the desired fullness, plus 4" (10 cm) for 1" (2.5 cm) double-fold side hems; cut one piece the width of the box spring times the desired fullness, plus 4" (10 cm) for 1" (2.5 cm) double-fold side hems. Dust ruffle depth is equal to distance from top of box spring to floor, plus 4" (10 cm).

For pleated bed skirt, cut deck 1" (2.5 cm) wider and 1" (2.5 cm) longer than box spring. Cut bed skirt on lengthwise grain of fabric. Cut two pieces the length of the box spring plus 18" (46 cm). Cut one piece the width of the box spring plus 18" (46 cm). Bed skirt depth equals distance from top of box spring to floor minus ¼" (6 mm) for clearance, plus 2½" (6.5 cm) for seam and hem.

YOU WILL NEED

Decorator fabric for dust ruffle or bed skirt.

Fitted sheet for deck of gathered dust ruffle.

Broadcloth, flat sheet or muslin for deck of pleated bed skirt.

How to Sew a Gathered Dust Ruffle with Open Corners

1) Stitch 1" (2.5 cm) double-fold hem along lower edges of the three dust ruffle pieces, then turn under and stitch 1" (2.5 cm) double-fold hem on both ends of each of the pieces.

2) Gather 1" (2.5 cm) from upper edge with ruffler attachment **(a)**, two-string shirring tape **(b)**, two rows of bastestitching **(c)**, or zigzag stitching over a cord **(d)**.

3) Place fitted sheet on box spring. On sheet, mark upper edge of box spring. Mark every 12" (30.5 cm) along this line. Mark upper edge of dust ruffle every 24" (61 cm) for double fullness, every 36" (91.5 cm) for triple fullness.

How to Sew a Pleated Bed Skirt

1) Fold deck in half lengthwise, then crosswise so corners are together. Using saucer as a guide, cut to curve corners gently.

2) Fold curved corners in half to determine centers; mark fold with ¼" (6 mm) clips. Also, mark center of each side with clip.

3) Stitch skirt pieces, right sides together, on narrow ends, with shorter piece in center. Stitch 1" (2.5 cm) double-fold hem on lower edge of skirt and on unstitched narrow ends of skirt pieces.

4) Pin right sides of dust ruffle pieces along three sides of sheet, raw edges on marked line and hems overlapping at corners. Match markings on dust ruffle pieces to markings on sheet. Pull up gathering cord to fit.

5) Remove sheet from box spring, keeping dust ruffle pinned in place. Stitch on gathering line, 1" (2.5 cm) from raw edge of dust ruffle.

6) Turn dust ruffle down over lower edge of sheet. If desired, topstitch ½" (1.3 cm) from seam, stitching through dust ruffle and sheet.

3" (7.5 cm)

3" (7.5 cm)

4) Pin skirt to deck, right sides together, with stitching of side hem at clip on one end of deck (arrow). Form 6" (15 cm) pleats at clips on sides and corners of deck. Seams will fall inside pleats.

5) Remove skirt and machine-baste pleats. Reposition skirt on deck. Pin, right sides together. Clip center of corner pleats. Stitch ½" (1.3 cm) seam.

6) Press seam allowance toward deck. Press ¼" (6 mm) double-fold hem at open end of deck; stitch hem. Topstitch the skirt seam allowance to deck. Press pleats.

Index